Anchors in Troubled Waters

HOW TO SURVIVE THE CRISES IN YOUR LIFE

BATSELL BARRETT BAXTER
HAROLD HAZELIP
JOE R. BARNETT

BAKER BOOK HOUSE
Grand Rapids, Michigan 49506

ISBN: 0-8010-0806-9

First printing, October 1981
Second printing, February 1982

Printed in the United States of America

Anchors in Troubled Waters

Foreword

> All the world's a stage,
> And all the men and women merely players:
> They have their exits and their entrances;
> And one man in his time plays many parts,
> His acts being seven stages.

These familiar words are found in Shakespeare's *As You Like It*, act 2, scene 7. In the lines that follow, Shakespeare tells about the infant, the schoolboy, the lover, the soldier, the justice, "the lean and slipper'd pantaloon," and second childhood.

Another author has referred to the stages of life in a more contemporary manner:

> We pass on from charming childhood to the tender teens; then from the teachable twenties into the tireless thirties; then the fiery forties and the forceful fifties; then come the serious sixties, the sober seventies, the aching eighties, and finally death, the sod, God!

Whatever method one may choose to describe the stages or periods of life, and no matter how challenging, exciting, happy, and rewarding each may be, it is certain that each period will have its crises.

At no stage in the life of an individual is there an absence of tension or turmoil. It is not easy for a baby to learn to walk, to talk, and to feed himself. As we look back on the early school years, we may be tempted to think of them as simple and idyllic, but if we do, it is because we have forgotten the tears and fears, the uncertainties and frustrations which punctuated the happy and rewarding childhood experiences. Later in life it is difficult to remember the depth of the anxieties of the teen years, but no teen-ager is unaware of their reality. So it is with each of the other periods of life.

Throughout our lives, as we face the crises which may seem overwhelming at the moment, we feel a need for help. That help often comes in the person of a family member, a teacher, a friend, or a professional. Sometimes we can solve our own problems. At other times we need to read and learn from others who have faced the same difficult situation and have successfully solved its intricacies. But for the deeper problems of life, there is one special source: the inspired Scriptures. So often, as we read and come to understand the principles which God has included in his divine Word, we see rays of light which provide the insights which help us know how to solve the problems in our lives.

Because we confidently believe that the truths of God have infinite value in helping us to survive the crises in each of our lives, we have brought together these messages which deal with some of the most serious trouble spots in life. While we have drawn on many sources for ideas and suggestions, we have found our greatest source of strength in the teachings of Christ, as found in the Bible. We offer them to you, as *Anchors in Troubled Waters*, with solid confidence that they can be of great help to you, for we have found them so in our own lives and in the lives of those about us.

Batsell Barrett Baxter
Harold Hazelip
Joe Barnett

Contents

1

Reducing Life's Stresses

Batsell Barrett Baxter

In recent years special television programs, articles in news magazines, and newspaper stories have highlighted examples of young executives who have retired from the pressures of city living to live on some remote farm. After earning a graduate degree in banking, or marketing, or advertising, a talented young executive must find life on the soil a strange experience indeed. Why would anyone cut himself off from friends and associates, a sizable income, and the comforts of modern living? The answer lies in the tremendous pressure which modern society often exerts on individuals and families. Such stress sometimes forces people to seek a permanent escape.

More of us choose the less extreme forms of escape. We work diligently through most of the months of the year in order to have two weeks of vacation at some remote hideaway. Our escape may be a camping trip with the family, or backpacking in one of the national parks, or flying to some warm-water, sun-drenched vacation spot. During the rest of the year there are the brief weekends when one flies to Colorado for skiing or simply breaks the routine by a few days away from the usual pressures.

There is something about wilderness areas which helps

us to recoup our losses. The stresses and strains of daily living are drained away as we drink in the beauty of mountain lakes, rushing streams, and stands of tall timber. Walking along a seashore, listening to the tides and the cry of the gulls, soothes away the strains.

Many of us sometimes find ourselves anxious and troubled about all the things we have to do. Many days are filled with little frustrations and stresses which leave us exhausted and emotionally drained at the end of the day. Then there are the larger stresses and strains which carry over from day to day and week to week, destroying our happiness and peace of mind. None of us are strangers to stress.

The Problem of Stress

More Americans die every year from coronary heart disease than from any other cause. Not long ago the Associated Press reported, "Heart disease is still the largest cause of death in the United States and accounted for 38 percent of the nation's nearly two million deaths last year." Many thoughtful people are saying that the number-one health problem—that which lies behind heart attacks, hypertension, high blood pressure, strokes, migraine headaches, and perhaps even cancer—is unbridled, uncontrolled stress. Many suggestions are being made: diet, avoidance of smoking and drinking, and the like. Exercise is being promoted widely. Everyone is talking about stress, its problems, and how to avoid it.

The "notion of stress" as a major health problem, according to *Psychology Today* in its March 1978 issue, was invented about forty years ago by Dr. Hans Selye, head of the International Institute of Stress at the University of Montreal. By definition, "stress is the body's non-specific response to any demand placed on it, whether that demand is pleasant or not." The effects are that "the endocrines, such as the pituitary located just under the brain, will produce a hormone which, in turn, stimulates the adrenal glands." The body is then prepared for flight or to fight. The "pulse races, breathing quickens, and the heart-beat soars." There is "a tendency to sweat, irritability, insomnia, less ability to concentrate, more movement, and the like." Dr. Selye writes, "We don't catch these types of illness—they happen to us because we are rendered vulnerable by the way we choose to live."

Dr. George Engle, professor of psychiatry and medicine at the University of Rochester School of Medicine, made a study of 275 cases of sudden death, as reported in newspaper accounts. His conclusion was that strong emotions often cause death. After careful analysis of each situation, he divided these 275 cases of sudden death into four categories: disruption of close personal relationships (135 cases); personal danger or a threat of injury or loss of life (103 cases); disappointment, failure, defeat, or loss of status (21 cases); and excited feelings of triumph or success (16 cases).

Characteristics of Modern Living

It is obvious that there is a great deal of stress in our world today. More personally, there is a great deal of stress in each of our lives. Do we have more stress today than in previous generations? Most of us would assume so; yet when one thinks of the pioneers who moved across the continent in covered wagons, constantly facing the threat of the Indians, inadequate water supplies, and all the other uncertainties of the trail, are we sure that we face more difficult situations today?

Modern living certainly has its stresses, too. A friend told me about living in the Washington, D.C., area during the time when Interstate 95, which passes the Pentagon, was under construction. Eventually there were twenty-six lanes of traffic on six levels. Thirty-five thousand people work in that one building each day. I also remember recently visiting the International Trade Center in New York and being told that 250,000 people either work in or visit those twin towers each day. Home situations also often bring stress. The mother who has the responsibility of caring for several children at home, with all of the other attendant responsibilities, inevitably feels stress in significant amounts. Situations like these—and there are many of them across the land—inevitably bring special pressures. Whether our stress is greater or less than the stress which the pioneers faced is of little significance. The fact is that we do have stress.

One might decide from this evidence that the best course of action is to find some way to avoid stress. However, this is impossible. To live in normal society is to have stress. We all have aims, desires, and goals that we wish to achieve in our lives. We also have obstacles and problems that frustrate those goals and create stress. The only solution is to learn to manage our stress so that it becomes a friend and not an enemy. If we learn to handle stress constructively, it will give us the very energy we need to overcome our problems.

What Can We Do About Stress?

Fortunately, there are some things that we can do about stress. Vacation or weekend retreats may be of some value, but they treat only the symptoms. Their benefits are fleeting at best. Exercise, changed diets, or giving up destructive habits are all helpful, but what we really need is to get to the root of the problem. Here are some fundamental suggestions.

First, we must recognize and understand the problem. What we have just been saying is a beginning. Hundreds of magazine articles and books deal with various aspects of the problem. At least a sampling of these is helpful. A few minutes in a good bookstore and the advice of a thoughtful salesperson can get us started. A few hours in a good library can give us the basic understanding we need. Then we are ready to move on to the basic steps which must be taken.

Second, we must get our priorities right. What most of us need is a better value system. We often spend our time in the pursuit of the wrong goals. We may also use methods which are ineffective. As sheep mindlessly following their leaders, many people live their lives with the primary emphasis on the pursuit of things. Fundamentally important relationships, such as those between husband and wife and parents and children, are sacrificed in order that the family's living standard may be kept high. A father takes a second job and is seldom at home with the family. A mother works outside the home, neglecting husband and children. While the house may be large and luxuriously furnished, while there may be two cars in the driveway, and while all the other evidences of affluent living may be present, the cost is extremely high.

Someone has said, "If you would be happy, keep your wants few and simple." There is a great deal to be said for this. Unhappiness comes when there is a gap between what we desire and what we have. Our modern system of advertising seems to say that happiness lies in having the newest, the best, the most luxurious of all kinds of things. But there is no way that anyone can have everything that he might conceivably want. If he would be happy he needs to control his wants and desires, keeping them in close range with what he has the ability to provide for himself.

Jesus once said, "It is written, 'Man shall not live by bread alone, but by every word that proceeds from the mouth of God" (Matt. 4:4). King Solomon sought the secret of happiness, much as modern man does, in the pursuit of power, pleasure, knowledge, and wealth, only to conclude at the end that all was "a striving after wind, and there was nothing to be gained under the sun" (Eccles. 2:11). His conclusion was, "The end of the matter; all has been heard.

Fear God, and keep his commandments; for this is the whole duty of man" (Eccles. 12:13).

Nothing can be more helpful in getting our priorities right than a thoughtful reading of God's Word. The entire Bible can be read in eighty-nine and one-half hours; the New Testament can be read in nineteen hours. A few minutes a day will take one through the entire Bible in a year. Such a reading would provide a clear understanding of the real goals of life. In the deepest sense, this is the place one must begin to reduce the stresses and strains of life. Only when we see clearly the goals for which life should be lived are we able to cut loose from the transient peripheral activities that so clutter and burden our lives.

Third, we must live according to right principles. Many people find their lives in turmoil because they violate daily the simple principles by which life must be lived if it is to run smoothly. They are constantly sawing against the grain, swimming upstream against the current. Take, for example, the simple matter of truthfulness. The person who has a low regard for telling the truth constantly finds himself in difficulties. It is impossible to remember, unless one is committed to tell the truth always and under all circumstances, exactly what one told this or that person yesterday or last week. He finds himself contradicting himself and destroying his credibility in the eyes of his associates. Those associates discover that they cannot trust him. How different it is with a person who is always and every time committed to telling the truth. He does not find himself in embarrassing situations. He does not have the strain of trying to remember what he told this person or that person.

Similarly the whole matter of honesty and integrity plays an important role in reducing life's stresses. The man who is absolutely honest, in little things as well as big things, never has to worry about being found out. Integrity elicits confidence and respect in others. Ethical behavior in business means that a person's employment is certain. Businesses thrive. Customers come.

When there is absolute honesty and complete integrity in family relationships there is a happiness that is beyond description. When a husband and wife trust each other completely they can enjoy life together, rather than constantly being nagged by doubts and suspicions. When children find that their parents are exactly what they claim to be they respect and love them. The opposite is devastating.

In the famous play *Death of a Salesman*, the two sons in the family idolized their father until they surprised him on a business trip one day and discovered that he was not faithful to their mother. After that, the relationships in the family were hollow.

The basic principles of Christianity, as taught in Christ's Sermon on the Mount and elsewhere throughout the New Testament, are essential if one is to have peace of mind. Honoring God, loving one's fellow men, maintaining an attitude of humble self-respect, and using things properly—these are the fundamentals of right living. The destructive emotions which fracture so many lives—fear, guilt, hatred, and feelings of failure—are not present. Life flows smoothly and the tensions and stresses are kept to a minimum.

Fourth, we must develop the spiritual side of life. Just as in ordinary living the absence of beautiful music, great literature, and travel leave a life impoverished, so the living of life on only the physical level leads to bankruptcy. Dr. Alexis Carrel, one of the world's most famous doctors and winner of a Nobel prize for physiology and medicine (1912), once wrote: "Despite its stupendous immensity, the world of matter is too narrow for man. Like his economic and social environment, it does not fit him. . . . With the aid of mathematical abstractions his mind apprehends the electrons as well as the stars. He is made on the scale of terrestrial mountains, oceans and rivers. . . . But he also belongs to another world. A world which, although enclosed within himself, stretches beyond space and time." He was speaking of the spiritual, inner nature of man, as was Augustine when he wrote, "Thou madest us for Thyself, and our heart is restless, until it repose in Thee."

The fact is that man essentially is not a physical body but an eternal soul. This is what is meant in Genesis 1:26–27, where God said, "Let us make man in our image, after our likeness; . . . So God created man in his own image, in the image of God he created him; male and female he created them."

Dr. Harold W. Bernard, a noted psychologist, in *Human Development in Western Culture*, states that human behavior is based on needs and then suggests this "hierarchy of needs":

1. physiological (food, clothing, shelter)
2. emotional (the need to love and to be loved)
3. social (the need for esteem, recognition, honor)
4. self-actualization (the need to fulfill one's nature)

It is this last need which is supremely important. The failure to achieve self-realization, remembering that we are made in the image of God, leads ultimately to a failure of life. This is reflected in a statement from Schopenhauer, "Man is never happy, but spends his whole life in striving after something which he thinks will make him so; he seldom attains his goal, and when he does it is only to be disappointed; he is mostly shipwrecked in the end, and comes into harbor with masts and rigging gone." This is a description of a spiritually barren life. How different it is with the Christian.

Fifth, we must trust God to take care of us. What a wonderful feeling of assurance the Christian has, even though he is in a world of vast uncertainties. It is a precarious world in which enemies invade, friends disappoint, accidents happen, diseases strike, everything runs down and wears out, and ultimately death conquers. How is it possible, in such a world, to survive without feelings of deep anxiety and despair?

The answer lies in the Christian's hope. Listen to Paul: "I know whom I have believed, and I am sure that he is able to guard until that Day what has been entrusted to me" (II Tim. 1:12). Hear him again as he says, "We are afflicted in every way, but not crushed; perplexed, but not driven to despair; persecuted, but not forsaken; struck down, but not destroyed . . ." (II Cor. 4:8–9). From a Roman prison, where he faced almost certain death at the hands of Caesar, he wrote, "Rejoice in the Lord always; again I will say, Rejoice. . . . Have no anxiety about anything, but in everything by prayer and supplication with thanksgiving let your requests be made known to God. And the peace of God, which passes all understanding, will keep your hearts and your minds in Christ Jesus. . . . I have learned, in whatever state I am, to be content. . . . I can do all things in him who strengthens me" (Phil. 4:4, 6–7, 11, 13).

As we come to believe in God as our Father and Jesus Christ as our Savior, we find an inner confidence which sustains us in all the crises of life. This identity—realizing that we are children of God, loved of God and protected by God—sustains us in every relationship of life. Then, too, there is a wonderful fellowship with other Christians who help us to bear our burdens and who share and thereby heighten our joys and happinesses. Most of all, our confidence is in Christ who lived on this earth, suffered the same kind of temptations and hardships we suffer, but conquered them all. In his last recorded words he said, "I am with you always" (Matt. 28:20).

Life has its stresses. There can be no mistake about that. But there is a way to handle those stresses, and that way is to follow in the steps of Christ, whose life with its beauty, strength, and serenity has changed the world. Paul once used the expression, "Have this mind among yourselves, which you have in Christ Jesus . . ." (Phil. 2:5). This is the secret of reducing life's stresses.

2

The Simple Life

Harold Hazelip

Divide the world into a rich one-third and a poor two-thirds. The rich one-third claims 87 percent of the gross world production each year. And the chasm between rich and poor is widening.

In the United States, the average energy usage per person is twice that of persons in West Germany or England. It is 350 times that of the average Ethiopian.

Our average food consumption is five times that of persons in the developing countries. Our beef consumption, for example, increased from 55 pounds per person in 1940 to 116 pounds per person in 1972.

We are an affluent society. Imagine the impression one of our shopping malls might make on a visitor from a less developed part of the world. There are busy crowds who have the leisure to "shop around." Advertisements offer suggestions for the "man who has everything." Well-dressed people look for new outfits.

People come to automobile show rooms looking for a new car with an extra touch of class. The television show room offers a TV with a sharper picture. What I believe would be amazing to this visitor is the insatiable appetite for buying by people who do not appear to be in need.

Our society, our economy, and our sense of self-esteem often seem to be built on discontent. Imagine what would happen if we were all to decide to keep the winter wardrobe and the car for an extra year, and that we love our home more than any house on the market.

Look through your favorite national magazine and notice how much of the magazine is composed of advertisements telling us that we lack something which is a necessity.

The ad tells you your home would be far more presentable if only you would get a new, elegant living-room suite. The style of last year's suit has been changed; even though the suit is in good condition, it would be a sign that you are not "keeping up" if you wear last year's style. Possessing things says something important to your friends. It tells them that you are doing well and keeping up with the latest trend.

Have you noticed that yesterday's luxuries are today's necessities? The result is that most of us now have "needs" we did not know we had until a few years ago. Let's raise a serious question about all this consumption. Is it really worth it to go on keeping up when we seem never to be satisfied with what we have?

The Price We Pay

Søren Kierkegaard told a parable about a wild dove in the forest. The wild dove lived near a farmer's house where there were some tame doves. The wild dove, which each day had to gather its own food, met one day with its relatives. The tame doves told how their needs were totally taken care of, and how each day the farmer provided them with food. The wild dove had never thought of itself as unfortunate until now. It had always trusted that its needs would be met in the forest. Now it was dissatisfied. The wild dove decided to slip into the farmer's barn through an opening. Never again would it have to find its own food.

The plan worked beautifully. But when the farmer came the next morning, he recognized the new dove immediately. He put it in a little box by itself until the next day, when it was killed—free from all anxiety for the necessities of life. We pay a big price with our discontent. If only the wild dove, which had always been provided for, had not been lured by its dissatisfaction to destroy itself!

I think of families I have known, and the price many of them have paid for their discontent. They bought new clothes when the style changed. They moved with each new raise. But there were pressures which went with all of the consuming. The father took a second job; the mother took her first. All of those purchases which they could not resist led to a dreadful pace of life. The children grew up almost by themselves. The parents seldom saw each other. When I think of them, I think of my enjoyment of a relaxed Saturday afternoon or holiday—which they seldom have.

Our society also pays for this consumption. Unstable home situations have an impact on schools. Families which have no time together leave us with unstable individuals who become a burden for others.

There is the price we pay when our throw-away mentality causes us to contaminate the place where we live with plastics, pollutants, and wastes—the 7 million junked cars each year, the 26 billion bottles, the 48 billion metal cans.

I doubt if any reasonable person believes that we can go on consuming indiscriminately forever. It appears to be an unavoidable fact that if we do not change our lifestyle and live on less, these changes will be forced on us. In *The Limits to Growth*, an international team of experts predicted that we will run out of many basic minerals and fuels early in the next century if we go on using resources as we have been. As we run out of those fuels and minerals, their prices will become higher and this style of life will become increasingly difficult to maintain. There will be a time when there are no more trees to cut, no more oil to pump, and no more natural resources to exploit.

A few years ago E. F. Schumacher wrote a provocative little book entitled *Small Is Beautiful.* He argued that our compulsive consumption is rooted in a spiritual crisis that afflicts the affluent society. Someone else has said that our discontent is caused by a basic boredom with life, a boredom that comes from having no other goals worth pursuing. Schumacher suggested that the only answer to this style of life is to be found in recovering spiritual roots that will help us overcome this discontent.

"Traveling Light"

When Jesus sent his disciples out on a mission, he charged them, "Take no gold, nor silver, nor copper in your belts, no bag for your journey, nor two tunics, nor sandals, nor a staff; for the laborer deserves his food" (Matt. 10:9–10). His advice, as his disciples were leaving on that preaching mission, was to "travel light." He knew that a great many possessions would be like a weight to slow them down. Perhaps taking every kind of provision would take away their trust in God. Jesus knew that we can easily be imprisoned by the things we own. What we possess then possesses us.

Jesus' advice about traveling light is helpful for the Christian life. The soldier knows that the cause he fights for is too important to allow him to be burdened by things he carries along. Pioneers never have the luxury of taking with them huge wardrobes; they have to select carefully. Christians also learn that their lives are a kind of pilgrimage toward the ultimate goal of the kingdom of God. They dare not take on any burdens that will interfere with their pilgrimage.

I was impressed by John V. Taylor's *Enough Is Enough.* Taylor observed that, despite the great beauty of a medieval cathedral, the grandeur of the cathedral symbolized wealth and power and esteem, if not downright human pride. He suggested that modern church builders not make the same mistake of building in grandeur; instead, churches should be simple structures. The church represents not wealth but the capacity to travel light.

Taylor went on to say that our homes should also reflect that we are Jesus' disciples who have taken the mission of traveling light. It is not necessary to abandon our homes; nor is it necessary to abandon our desire for beauty, space, rest, and warmth. Yet these desires should not possess us. "It is better not to have a carpet," Taylor says, "than to have one we cannot bear to see trodden by dirty shoes." Couldn't we say the same about our automobiles, our clothes, and our entertainment? To travel light does not mean abandoning all of these things and retiring to the desert. But it does mean not being so burdened by them that we cannot carry on the mission for which we have been sent.

A nineteenth-century story from Kierkegaard again illustrates this point. A prosperous man, on a dark but starlit night, drives comfortably with the lanterns of his carriage shining brightly. As he goes along he is safe; he fears no difficulty. Because he carries his light with him wherever he goes, it is never dark in his presence. Yet because he has those strong lights close to him, he cannot see the stars. The poor peasant driving without lights can see the beautiful stars. So we may become occupied with the necessities of life. In our prosperity and good days, everything is so satisfactory, so pleasant, so comfortable. But the view is lacking—the view of the stars.

It was this perspective that Jesus did not want us to lose. He did not demand that all of his disciples give up their property; indeed, we are told about Simon Peter's home and about wealthy women who gave money to support Jesus. But Jesus did demand that we keep our perspective. If we seek only the glittering lights of the shopping mall, we will never see the stars. "But seek first his kingdom and his righteousness, and all these things shall be yours as well" (Matt. 6:33). The culture in which Jesus lived had perhaps as much discontent as our own. He saw the anxiety in the faces of the crowd, an anxiety rooted in a lack of trust in God. But he called on his people to travel light. "The Gentiles seek all these things," he said (Matt. 6:32).

Resisting the Pull of Greed

The center of Jesus' message was bound up with the conviction that his people have resources to resist the pull of greed. He told a story about a merchant who found a costly pearl, and then sold all that he had in order to have the one thing. He told of a treasure found in a field and the merchant who sold all that he had in order to have it. On another occasion a man came to Jesus and said, "Teacher, bid my brother divide the inheritance with me" (Luke 12:13). But Jesus replied, "Take heed, and beware of all covetousness; for a man's life does not consist in the abundance of his possessions" (Luke 12:15). Then Jesus told the story of the rich farmer whose life was so caught up with the pursuit of wealth that he tore down his barns in order to build greater ones. But he paid a price for his greed, for God said to him, "Fool! This night your soul is required of you" (Luke 12:20). By not traveling light, the man had gotten things out of perspective.

I spoke earlier about the sense of discontent in our society. I think of the apostle Paul, as he wrote to the Philippians from prison in Rome. He was awaiting the sentence on his life. He had known his share of deprivation, inconvenience, and humiliation. He wrote, "Not that I complain of want; for I have learned, in whatever state I am, to be content. I know how to be abased, and I know how to abound; in any and all circumstances I have learned the secret of facing plenty and hunger, abundance and want. I can do all things in him who strengthens me" (Phil. 4:11–13). Paul had found the resource for doing without.

Paul regularly warned against the evils of covetousness, or, literally, "wanting more and more." He wrote to new Christians, "Then put to death those parts of you which belong to the earth—fornication, indecency, lust, foul cravings, and the ruthless greed which is nothing less than idolatry" (Col. 3:5, NEB). When he faced situations in which there was need among Christians, he devoted years of his ministry taking up a collection for the benefit of the poorer churches.

Not all of the early Christians gave up their property. But in Jesus Christ they found the mission that so captivated them that nothing else mattered. Paul put it this way, "From now on, let those who . . . buy [live] as though they had no goods, and those who deal with the world as though they had no dealings with it" (I Cor. 7:29–31). Their new life in Christ did not mean that they no longer had possessions, but it did give them a new distance from their possessions.

One writer suggests that Christians have been forceful and clear in treating some teachings of the Bible without taking a firm stand with all parts of it. There may be truth in this charge. It is tempting to be firm with the Bible's demands for sexual morality and honesty toward our neighbors and yet be caught up in the pressures to consume far more than we need. John Taylor says, in *Enough is Enough*, that the Christian's greatest opportunity and challenge is presented in living out the words of Jesus relating to possessions. "It is not enough to talk," Taylor says. "Western societies are sick of moralizing about world poverty. We need a thoughtful, convinced minority that will *live* in such a way as to challenge the beliefs of the consumer society and defy its compulsions." We need, Taylor tells us, a "joyful resistance movement" that refuses to be manipulated by the trend setters or follow the ambitions that are expected of them.

I frequently read about some "resistance movement" which rejects the consumer society and attempts to retreat to a simpler life. The hippie movement and various communes have tried their own versions of a "counter-culture." But I suspect that they lack the resources for traveling light for a long time. I believe that Jesus Christ has allowed us to see the goals which give us the strength to "seek first his kingdom and his righteousness . . ." (Matt. 6:33). We who have a mission can indeed travel light.

3
Overcoming Hostility

Batsell Barrett Baxter

The morning newspaper and the evening news report tell us about the day's events. Many of these reports inform us about violence: assault, murder, armed robbery, rape, assassination, and global skirmishes. All of these are symptoms of a society which has experienced rampant hostility.

Of the four major destructive emotions—fear, guilt, hostility, and failure—hostility is the worst. Only the dramatic or tragic acts of hostility make the headlines. We don't hear much about the friendships, the working relationships, or the families which are being torn apart by hostility. This tragic situation will continue until we learn that hostility is like an acid which does greater damage to the container in which it is stored than the object on which it is poured.

Causes of Hostility

Some people blame television for the increasing violence in our midst, feeling that the instant, full-color presentation of violent scenes from every corner of the earth serves to advertise and encourage violence. There is some truth in this. However, these widespread acts of hostility are only symptoms of a deeper problem. Advertising violence may tend to spread it, but only because beneath the surface there are already the seeds of violence among many people in many places.

Depersonalization of the individual has been one of the negative results of both the technological age and the population explosion. When a person feels himself to be an unimportant, unnoticed cog in a great wheel, he is likely to feel resentment. In our era people also seem to be more suspicious of one another and to trust and depend less on one another. Many view the world in which they live as unjust. Some live with constant fear and anxiety. Others are frustrated and hurting inside. These and other feelings like them are among the main causes of widespread anger. Anger can easily become hostility and hostility often erupts into violence.

Anger is an emotion. Dr. S. I. McMillen, in *None of These Diseases*, points out, "Our emotions are neither good nor bad. It is their use or misuse which makes them positive or destructive." There is probably no way to live very long in our modern, complex world without feeling anger. When some goal or purpose to which we have set ourselves is suddenly blocked, anger flares. You see it in the child from whom a toy is taken. You see it in a man when the fender of his car is crushed and his progress is delayed. The real question is not whether anger will come, but what we do with the emotion when it arises.

I think the Bible recognizes the reality of what I have just been saying, for the apostle Paul wrote, "Be angry but do not sin" (Eph. 4:26). There may be no way to avoid feelings of anger, but we can learn to handle those feelings constructively rather than destructively.

Tragic Results

Some people feel that hostility and anger are the same. But there is a vast difference between the two. Hostility is anger which is being expressed with vengeance. Hostility may explode outwardly in violence, as it so often does, or it may turn inward, nurturing grudges or feelings of hatred. Neither expression of anger is constructive: violence may result in the destruction of property, the loss of a job, or even a murder, followed by years spent in prison. When turned inward, hostility may result in a variety of unfortunate mental attitudes and all kinds of physical ailments. The person expressing hatred or harboring grudges often reaps the consequences of his hostility to a far greater degree than those whom he hates.

A doctor friend of mine, a few years ago, described two farmers who had a falling out over a relatively unimportant matter—one man's cows occasionally strayed into the other man's field. The man whose field had been violated developed a hatred for his neighbor that eventually caused stomach ulcers. This man would have problems with his ulcers, stay in the hospital a few days, and then go home. On one occasion when his neighbor's cows got into his field, he shot two of them. In court, he had to pay the damages. This resulted in such a flare-up of his ulcers that he died. My doctor concluded by saying that tragically, over a period of twenty years, this farmer had committed suicide—the slow, hard way—out of hatred for his neighbor.

Recently I noticed a bumper sticker saying, "I don't get mad, I get even." This has also been used as a motto for T-shirts. How easy it is when we feel that we have been put down, or wronged, or ridiculed, or even just ignored, to have the desire to "get even." Our pride has been hurt. Our rights must be protected. Therefore, we want to get even. But the price is very high. As Dr. McMillen puts it, "Man doesn't seem to learn that the high cost of getting even may be toxic goiter, strokes of apoplexy, and fatal heart attacks." He goes on to say, "The verbal expression of animosity toward others calls forth certain hormones from the pituitary, adrenal, thyroid, and other glands, an excess of which can cause disease in any part of the body."

Nation's Business recently told of this tragic example of the effects of anger which was allowed to become hostility: A board of inquiry blamed Britain's worst air disaster on a pilot who suffered a heart attack just before his plane crashed. The 118 persons aboard were killed. The board's report stated that "the heart attack stemmed from a heated argument in the airline's crew room just before the flight. It is clear that the pilot was very angry indeed. It is likely that the blood vessels of the heart had already been weakened by the stress from previous bouts of hostility."

Some Values

Even though anger has negative aspects, it has also served the interests of man's survival through many centuries. Anger energizes us for attack, just as fear energizes us for flight. The problem, as we have seen, is how to control our anger.

Booker T. Washington, the black educator, was sometimes a victim of animosity and injustice created by bigotry. When others treated him unjustly he said, "I will not let any man reduce my soul to the level of hatred." Of course, Washington experienced anger; however, he was wise enough to deal with his anger appropriately. Someone else has said, "The moment I start hating a man I become his slave. He controls me."

It has been established that anger as an emotion is neither good nor bad. When handled appropriately it is a positive force. Misused it becomes destructive. This leads to a critical question: Are there any guidelines to follow so that our anger will become a positive part of our personalities rather than a destructive part? In answering this question we want to look at four ways in which to deal with anger.

Four Ways of Dealing with Anger

The four possible ways of dealing with anger are to repress it, suppress it, express it, or confess it. Notice first the repression of anger. This means simply to put the anger out of one's conscious mind and to force it into the subconscious mind. This is often the easiest and most immediate way to deal with anger, yet its consequences can be severe. Dr. Cecil G. Osborne writes: "A major cause of severe depression is repressed hostility. . . . For instance, a mistreated or unloved child feels a mixture of hurt and anger. If he learns early in life that anger is forbidden, he acquires the habit of burying his feelings to win parental approval and avoid punishment. In repressing his natural anger, he lays the groundwork for depression. Later he may become a pleasant, self-contained, placid personality totally unaware of the repressed anger deep within himself. But his body is aware of it, and responds with depression, or in many cases with physical symptoms. . . . Repression takes a terrible toll and is the source of some of our most troublesome physical problems. . . ."

In the second place, suppression of anger can have bad consequences. While repression of anger is putting it from our consciousness, the suppression of anger is to consciously hold our anger inside. The danger of this is that continual suppression of anger may ultimately "boil over." So much pressure and hostility builds up inside that when it is finally expressed it is usually so explosive that it is destructive. People who suppress their anger are often human examples of Mount St. Helens. It is also possible to continue to suppress anger indefinitely, which results in serious internal turmoil.

A third way of dealing with anger is to express it in a negative, destructive way, that is, to "blow up" or to retaliate. For many years some behavioral scientists have argued that it is unhealthy to try to control feelings of animosity. Descriptive terminology such as "therapeutic aggression," "catharsis," "ventilation," or "leveling" is often used. Encounter groups and sensitivity groups which have gained widespread popularity in the past decade often use these theories. Participants are encouraged to vent their feelings in some activity. If you have feelings of hatred toward a person you might be told to hit a pillow repeatedly, while thinking that you are actually hitting the hated person. This may sound wonderful at first, but actually it is very misleading.

Leonard Berkowitz, the famed psychologist, comments, "Experimental psychologists, by and large, are skeptical of the energy theory that underlies ventilation therapies . . . depending upon the circumstances, a person's inhibitions might be lowered or his aggressive behavior might be reinforced, increasing the chances that the person will act aggressively outside the therapy situation." He goes on to say, "I do not think it is necessary to act out one's hostility. . . . We can talk about our feelings and describe our emotional reactions without attacking others verbally or physically, directly or in fantasy." Research has shown that ventilation can increase aggressive behavior.

The Only Good Way

The fourth and only good way to handle anger is by developing a new nature or way of looking at life. In an important passage in his letter to the Ephesians, the apostle Paul wrote, "Put off your old nature which belongs to your former manner of life and is corrupt through deceitful lusts, and be renewed in the spirit of your minds, and put on the new nature, created after the likeness of God in true righteousness and holiness" (Eph. 4:22–24).

Paul, unlike the ventilationists, insists that the "natural man" must not be given free rein. The old pagan nature can be put off only by putting on the new nature. The new nature is the new power and lifestyle which can only be found in relationship with Jesus Christ. At the center of one's life is a new value system and a new way of thinking about one's self, other people, and material things.

Paul continued, "Therefore, putting away falsehood, let every one speak the truth with his neighbor, for we are members one of another. Be angry but do not sin; do not let the sun go down on your anger, and give no opportunity to the devil" (Eph. 4:25–27). This reveals that the proper way to handle our anger is to be truthful about our feelings, confessing the anger we are experiencing. Then we should deal with it within that day. The reason is so that the devil will not gain a foothold. Anger which is not confessed can easily become bitterness and bitterness leads to hostility.

An example of this is found in Genesis 4. Cain became angry with his brother Abel. The text states, "Cain was very angry, and his countenance fell" (Gen. 4:5). The Lord warned Cain that he must control his temper for sin was "couching at the door" (v. 7). In other words, if Cain would not appropriately deal with his anger that anger would become sinful. Cain failed to confess his anger. Harboring his bitterness ultimately led to the first murder.

In the Sermon on the Mount, Jesus made several statements about relationships with others. He states that anger with a person which results in verbal abuse is as bad as murder (Matt. 5:21–26). He later warns against retaliation in Matthew 5:38–42. Then he says, "You have heard that it was said, 'You shall love your neighbor and hate your enemy.' But I say to you, Love your enemies and pray for those who persecute you, so that you may be sons of your Father who is in heaven; for he makes his sun rise on the evil and on the good, and sends rain on the just and on the unjust. For if you love those who love you, what reward have you? . . . And if you salute only your brethren, what more are you doing than others? . . . You, therefore, must be perfect, as your heavenly Father is perfect" (Matt. 5:43–46, 47, 48). The perfection we are called to is that of unconditional love for others. We are to love, that is, seek the other's highest good even when he or she does not deserve it. God loved us and gave his Son for us when we did not deserve it. John wrote, "If God so loved us, we also ought to love one another" (I John 4:11).

Paul wrote in similar terms in Romans 12:17–21. "Repay no one evil for evil, but take thought for what is noble in the sight of all. If possible, so far as it depends upon you, live peaceably with all. Beloved, never avenge yourselves, but leave it to the wrath of God; for it is written, 'Vengeance is mine, I will repay, says the Lord.' No, 'if your enemy is hungry, feed him; if he is thirsty, give him drink; for by so doing you will heap burning coals upon his head.' Do not be overcome by evil, but overcome evil with good."

The Christian Way

In summary I would like to stress that retaliation is an inappropriate way to express our anger. Also, to suppress or to repress anger has bad consequences. However, anger can be expressed appropriately. I have referred to this as confession. It involves honestly admitting our anger without attacking the source. This allows for a rational analysis of the situation. It also increases the possibility of the situation being resolved. It is urgent that we follow the biblical directives. We must confess our anger within the same day that it arises, lest it develop into bitterness and hatred.

Finally, it is obvious that if we accept this dramatic and challenging approach to the handling of anger—the developing of a new nature and outlook on life—it involves a close relationship with the Lord Jesus Christ. We cannot do it on our own. We need his guidance and his strength. This means that we need to be Christians. Not only does Christ's new way of life help us master the problems that grow out of feelings of anger, but it also helps us conquer all of our other human problems as well. The happiest, best way to live is the Christian way.

4

Attacking the Agony of Loneliness

Joe R. Barnett

Loneliness. That must be the most desolate word in human language. It plays no favorites, ignores all rules of courtesy, extends no mercy.

Loneliness. It comes uninvited . . . and stays . . . and stays . . . and stays.

There is no agony more painful than the consuming anguish of loneliness. The inmate in prison can tell you that, or the serviceman in a foxhole, or a bar, thousands of miles from home. So can the divorceé in a lonely apartment, or the person who has just buried a companion. So can the couple whose hearts ache for the child recently taken, or the single person who prepares a meal for one and goes to bed early, alone, surrounded by the mute memory of "what might have been."

I think of the elderly widow, who puts up a brave front, but who lives alone with only pictures of past companionships. I think of the young widow for whom life looked so bright—until a sudden accident. Now she has gone back to her hometown to try to pick up the pieces and start over.

I think of the 68-year-old woman who spent a busy life rearing her children. Then they were gone. She said, "I can clean my house in a very short time. Then I have nothing to do. *No one really needs me.*"

There was the alcoholic who wept with such remorse, and so hopelessly, clutching in his fist the note left by his wife and children, "Goodby, forever."

There was the young husband standing beside a fresh grave, sobbing, "What now?"

There was the disillusioned teen-age girl, far away from home and heavy with child, wondering, "How can I face tomorrow?"

Is there anything we can do to combat loneliness?

Some time ago this ad appeared in a Midwestern newspaper:

> I will listen to you talk for 30 minutes without a comment for $5.

Sounds like a hoax, doesn't it? But it wasn't. The person who placed the ad received ten to twenty calls a day. The pang of loneliness is so sharp that some people are willing to try anything for a half-hour of companionship.

A Nation of Strangers

Loneliness shows no partiality. It attacks the laborer who faithfully works in the shop and is seldom recognized for anything—except when he is absent.

Loneliness strikes out at the chief executive officer of that company. He has to be tough, has to keep things going, and has to work longer hours than anyone else. His phone rings constantly and there's an endless flow of traffic through his office. But he's lonely. He's learned the hard way to be suspicious of offers of friendship. As one top executive said, "I want to eat with them, laugh with them, be one of them. Instead, we meet, we speak, we pass each other—I do my act, they applaud, and that's it." It's lonely at the top.

The only solution to loneliness seems to be company. Yet, paradoxically, crowds may increase our loneliness. This was Simon and Garfunkel's description of city life in "The Sounds of Silence."

Flight to the city in search of new jobs and expanded opportunities has brought us closer to others than we have ever been. We may live in an apartment house with five hundred other families. We can hear through the thin walls—the family quarrel, the television, the vacuum.

We are jammed together on the freeway, the bus, and the elevator. Everywhere we turn there are people, masses of people.

We are, as Vance Packard wrote, *A Nation of Strangers.* Our fathers and grandfathers lived in communities where there was a supportive network of relatives and friends. They knew each other at the grocery store, the blacksmith shop, and the doctor's office. They knew each other at work and on the adjoining farm. But much of this has changed. We may not even know our neighbor's name.

Paul Tournier tells of a Swiss woman who lived in a large apartment house and worked in a shop with many people. Every evening she tuned in to the sign-off of the radio station just to hear a voice say, "We wish you a very pleasant good night." She imagined that voice speaking just to her. She hungered for a *personal* greeting even though she heard hundreds of voices each day.

We were meant to live with others. As John Donne said, "No man is an island." God said it better: "It is not good that man should be alone" (Gen. 2:18).

Psychiatrist Harry Stack Sullivan has said that the deepest problems of our society are loneliness, isolation, and the inability to have self-esteem.

A Clever Enemy

Loneliness strikes hard and doesn't play fair. It tells us we are unappreciated and ill-treated.

Loneliness is a clever enemy. It slips into the office of the hard worker who has been ignored and bypassed for promotion and twists his mind with self-pity.

Loneliness sneaks into the hospital room and says to the sick person, "You've been forgotten. No one cares about you—not really."

To the unemployed loneliness says, "No chance!" To the divorced it says, "No place!" To the bereaved it says, "No hope!" To the struggling it says, "No way!"

Loneliness is hard to deal with. It throws us into a vicious circle, causing feelings of self-doubt, which in turn bring on deeper loneliness. And it may persist until there's almost a complete loss of self-worth.

Feeling that no one understands or cares, we may retreat into a shell of self-pity and isolation. Gloom settles, and hopelessness. We feel trapped. There doesn't seem to be any way out.

Solutions for Loneliness

There aren't any simple solutions, but here are some things which should help.

First, don't be too hard on yourself. When loneliness clutches us there's a tendency to feel something is lacking in our character. This isn't necessarily so.

The roster of the lonely in the Bible looks like a list in *Who's Who.* It includes David, Jeremiah, Job, Moses, John the Baptist, and Paul. And don't you know Mary, the mother of Jesus, was terribly lonely when she was awaiting the birth of Jesus—and people were whispering about her "condition"?

Elijah is a classic example of a person suffering that deep, want-to-die kind of loneliness. He even said, "It is enough; now, O LORD, take away my life" (I Kings 19:4). That's about as low as you can get.

What was wrong? Elijah felt he was alone. Listen to him: "I have worked very hard for the Lord God of the heavens; but the people of Israel have broken their covenant with you and torn down your altars and killed your prophets, and only I am left . . ." (I Kings 19:10, LB).

There you have it. Elijah felt alone, unloved, and unappreciated. He felt totally isolated. Nobody was with him, not even God!

But do you know what? It wasn't long before Elijah was living a happy, victorious life again. How did he do it? If you're lonely, read this carefully. From this story comes a four-step program for overcoming loneliness.

Keep physically fit. This was the first step for Elijah. God encouraged him to get a good night's sleep and eat a good meal or two (I Kings 19:5–6).

We easily slide into a low mood when we're tired. If you are seriously ill there may not be much you can do about it. But doing the best you can to keep *physically* fit will go a long way toward keeping you *mentally* positive.

Verbalize your frustration. Elijah wasn't talking to anyone. He went out into the wilderness and hid in a cave. Loneliness often drives us deeper into isolation. We avoid the very people whose company could eliminate our loneliness.

When God finally forced Elijah to talk, Elijah poured out his frustration: "I've tried to do right. I've tried to be good. And yet, I'm alone. No one is on my side." This was a "poor me, what-have-I-done-to-deserve-this" speech. But that was all right. God let Elijah talk, because Elijah needed to get his feelings out in the open.

That's a good pattern. Verbalizing a problem is a big part of the solution.

Get busy; get involved. God told Elijah, "Go . . . anoint Hazael . . . and Jehu . . . and Elisha . . ." (vv. 15–16).

God was assuring Elijah that he had a future. "Elijah, it's time for you to get back to work. I need you. I have something I want you to do."

Idleness is fertile ground for loneliness. Activity, even when forced, is a key to mind control.

Get a fresh view of God. When God asked Elijah why he was isolating himself, licking his wounds, and feeling sorry for himself, Elijah spit out his feelings. The last thing he said was, "*only I am left*" (italics mine).

There it is—that feeling of being alone and not having anyone who understands or appreciates you.

Loneliness spills over into our feelings about God. Elijah had seen God do some powerful things. But God didn't seem to be working now, and Elijah was wondering, "How could God let this happen to me?"

Sometimes we feel that way. But God's care was forever proved through Jesus. More than anything else, you need to know that Jesus wants to be your friend during times of loneliness.

Look at what Jesus did! He became like us in order to befriend us. So he could understand our feelings he came and experienced the same life cycle and the same feelings which are ours. He faced the same temptations we face; put himself in our shoes. The writer of Hebrews summed it up: "we have not a high priest who is unable to sympathize with our weaknesses, but one who in every respect has been tempted as we are . . ." (Heb. 4:15).

You're lonely? He knows. He cares. He understands. He is touched. He is moved.

If you feel God doesn't know and doesn't care, or that you're not getting through to him, or that for some unexplainable reason he has forsaken you, you have an ally in Jesus. That's the way he felt. As he faced the cross, he cried out, "My God, my God, why hast thou forsaken me?" (Matt. 27:46). In the strangling grip of the cross he experienced the maximum impact of loneliness.

So Jesus is able to sympathize with you and go into the battle with you when you have to fight the giant of Loneliness. You don't have to explain—he already knows. He needs only an invitation to share the wound and to help the healing.

More than anything else, when you are lonely you need an understanding friend. Jesus is the one—perhaps the only one—who can really understand.

Jesus had to die alone. As he explained to his disciples, "The hour is coming, indeed it has come, when you will be scattered, every man to his home, and will leave me alone; yet I am not alone, for the Father is with me" (John 16:32).

Jesus offers the same presence to you. There will still be moments of loneliness after you have committed your life to him, but not like the painful loneliness you've experienced before having him as your friend.

And you can have him as a friend. He said, "You are my friends if you do what I command you" (John 15:14). Obey those commands, and claim his friendship.

5

Surviving Depression

Batsell Barrett Baxter

We have always been good at labeling the spirit of an age with a one- or two-word description. There were the gay nineties and the roaring twenties. We remember the 1930s especially for the depression, and the 1940s for the war. The 1950s have been remembered as the placid decade, and the 1960s the age of activism. We have barely left the 1970s, and the journalists are still looking for the right word to describe that period.

The word that we are hearing most often, however, to describe the 1970s is "apathy." We left the activist decade and entered the apathetic decade. Psychologist Karl Menninger has said that our whole society is suffering from depression. One newspaper editor asked, "What ails the American spirit?" The answer he most often heard was, "Collective despair." The problems of our complicated world are too big for us. Solutions are not keeping up with the problems.

If our age is a period of collective depression, it is reasonable that this translates into millions of individuals who suffer from depression. Long ago, Thoreau spoke of the many who "live lives of quiet desperation." I wonder what he would say today if he were to see the seriousness of the problem which Western society has with alcoholism and drug abuse.

Most people begin their lives with idealistic hopes. They dream many dreams of success in various fields. Many youngsters are "superstars" in their fantasies. Happy marriages, large incomes, elegant homes, and all the rest are assumed or taken for granted. Then things go wrong and these dreams have to be filed away one by one. The result: depression. Disillusionment, hopelessness, and despair follow. This is especially true if there is serious illness, or the breakup of a meaningful marriage, or the loss of an important job, or some other life-shaking experience.

Defining the Problem

Exactly what is depression? While many factors contribute to feelings of depression, the basic element is a feeling of helplessness. Depression comes when a person faces a situation which he feels is beyond his power to handle. The situation seems hopeless. Unfortunately this feeling of helplessness is widespread, touching all levels of society. Older people feel depression, but it is also known among youth. The rich and the poor, the educated and the uneducated, the famous and the unknown—all are victims of depression. Sometimes the depression is deep enough to be psychotic, in which case a professional physician needs to be called on for help. Simple depression, or a severe case of the "blues," often responds to one's own intelligent efforts to leave the despondent mood behind. Many people, however, instead of making valiant efforts to overcome feelings of depression, resort to escapes, such as alcohol, travel, constant activity, or other such devices.

Usually depression grows out of some loss. It may be the result of the loss of a spouse or of children leaving home. The loss of a job or retirement can bring on depression. Sometimes it is the result of the letdown which follows the realization of some great goal or achievement. The decline of abilities with age often triggers feelings of depression. The loss of a home by fire, or the failure of a business, or the theft of one's valuables can lead to depression.

There are common symptoms of depression which may go unnoticed, but actually are quite obvious. Psychological factors are a tendency to withdraw from society, feelings of self-condemnation, or critical attitudes toward others. There also may be physical symptoms such as a general feeling of apathy and lack of energy. A whole range of minor physical problems and even some major illnesses may be caused by mental attitudes of depression and despair.

What Can Be Done?

The place to begin is inside one's self. The depressed person needs to pause and remember that he is a human being made in the image of God and, therefore, is important. It is important to think back to one's achievements and successes. It is healthy to recognize one's own importance. One of the best ways to do this is to remember the clear teachings in the Bible concerning God's love for each individual. In depression the self-image has been damaged and needs to be restored.

The second step is to remember that external circumstances do not control us. We are creatures of choice and have the power of rising above difficult environments. A case in point is George Frederick Handel, who was old and blind and whose wife had recently died when he composed his masterpiece, the *Messiah*, which contains the inspiring and uplifting "Hallelujah Chorus." Everything about Handel's situation was discouraging, yet he rose to the heights in this magnificent musical composition which has blessed the lives of countless thousands since.

In the third place, depression tends to be dispelled when a person turns his attention outward. The moment that he begins to think of other people, he begins to forget his own problems. If he can become involved in helping other people then he has likely won his battle against depression. Self-centeredness leads to depression; concern for others overcomes depression.

Still another suggestion is physical conditioning. Exercising, eating the right foods, and getting adequate rest all help overcome the negative feelings of discouragement. Often depression is a result of poor health. As health improves, the feelings of discouragement leave.

Finally, surrounding one's self with positive, constructive people is a step toward overcoming depression. Enthusiastic people help one forget his own feelings of discouragement. A retiring, depressed person may be well advised to get a job which would require going out among people daily. Laughter is better than medicine. Laughter lifts the spirits and makes it difficult to be discouraged.

These are a few special practical suggestions for overcoming depression. When practiced they will have an almost immediate effect in helping one climb out of the pit of despair in which he may find himself. It may be helpful to examine some real cases of depression in order to see some of the factors that led to the condition and some of the ways that depression might have been avoided.

An Intangible Loss

In *Coping With Crises*, Ruth Fowke tells about a young man who had just left college with a degree and obtained a job that he had always wanted. He had every reason to be on top of the world, yet he became unaccountably depressed. At first his friends were concerned and sympathetic, but as time went by and he showed no sign of emerging from his melancholy state, they began to lose patience with him—as he did with himself.

This case study illustrates the various ways that depression comes. Depression is related to a loss, but sometimes the loss is rather intangible. It may be the loss of a loved one, or it may be, quite simply, the loss of a dream, the feeling that the future has nothing to offer. Depression may come at the moment of the biggest triumph, just as we see that there appears to be nothing beyond the mountains we have climbed. The young man in this story seemed to have everything that he had dreamed of, yet inwardly there was an emptiness which led to depression.

A Biblical Example

There is a remarkable case study of this kind of depression in the Bible. If anyone had reason to feel on top of the world, it was Elijah. In a story that is recorded in I Kings, Elijah had just finished one of his greatest triumphs. The victory could not have been more spectacular. There was a thrilling contest on Mount Carmel between Elijah and the false prophets of King Ahab and Queen Jezebel, in which God destroyed the forces of Baal. Strangely, it was after this great triumph, this extremely high moment in his life, that Elijah reached the depths. In I Kings 19 we read, "Then he was afraid, and he arose and went for his life, and came to Beer-sheba, which belongs to Judah, and left his servant there. But he himself went a day's journey into the wilderness, and came and sat down under a broom tree; and he asked that he might die, saying, 'It is enough; now, O LORD, take away my life; for I am no better than my fathers' " (vv. 3–4). Elijah had given up in despair and had run away to the southernmost part of the land. Emotionally and physically exhausted, he lay down to sleep.

The symptoms of depression are here. There is the letdown following the great moment which had drawn all of Elijah's energies. With the coming of a feeling that there was no future, his energies had slipped away and there was an awful lethargy. He was ready to die.

Elijah thought he was alone, yet God spoke of seven thousand who had been faithful. Notice especially, however, that God deals with this discouraged, despondent man by giving him work to do. God sends Elijah back and gives him a task to perform. The result is that Elijah came out of his depression and continued to serve Jehovah in a fine way.

Let's take a few moments to examine this story to see what caused Elijah to become so despondent. In this story there are several significant elements which may have a bearing on our lives. First, Elijah did much to cause the problem himself. He took his eyes off God and placed them on himself. As Elijah's gloom was due in part to his having run away from God, so also our low times may be a result of turning our backs on God.

Second, Elijah apparently expected too much of himself. He was intent on trying to be perfect, which inevitably leads to feelings of failure and inferiority. He said, "I am no better than my fathers." This really means, "I have accomplished no more than my fathers." When we realize that we are not what we want to be or ought to be, we may feel discouragement and depression.

Third, Elijah's depression came when he was tired and hungry. Our physical condition may be a major factor in our feelings of discouragement from time to time. Our physical feelings sometimes overpower our spiritual nature, so it is wise to take care of our bodies in order that our spirits may be in health.

Fourth, Elijah felt an overpowering loneliness. He had the impression that he was the only one in all of Israel who was loyal to Jehovah. This sometimes may be the source of our frustration. Like Elijah, we sometimes need to open our eyes and see the many fine faithful people about us.

Finally, Elijah's problem was a lack of trust in God. Elijah took much on himself, feeling that he was the one who had the responsibility of triumphing over the idolatrous people around him. If he had trusted in God, realizing that while he himself was weak God was infinitely strong, this story would never have been written. Let us have patience when we are discouraged, remembering that God is still in his heaven and that his power is infinite.

Encouraging Suggestions

It appears that depression lingers on those who concentrate for a long time on their own feelings and look inward only. Psychologists tell us that working through depression involves recognizing once more that the world offers challenges. Once we learn to forget ourselves, we are on the path of recovery from depression. When we then find a job that is worth doing, and trust God to help us be equal to our task, we begin to move out of our feelings of frustration and despair.

In the role of counselor, I have seen a number of instances in which people have faced tragedies which were followed by despair. I recall one instance in which a young man who had been only nominally involved in church life was abandoned by his wife and left more lonely than he had ever been. The people of the church flowed to meet his needs and provided strength and encouragement. Later he commented, "You saved my life."

I recall instances of young women who were left widowed in unexpected and tragic circumstances. They found in the church a source of strength which they had never before realized. I know of retired people who are investing their energies in the life of the church and thus avoiding the "retirement syndrome" which comes to many who are left depressed, lonely, and with nothing to do. I have seen those who were stricken by serious illness lifted up and sustained by Christian friends. In Elijah's story it was the angel who brought the depressed prophet his food and drink when he was so absorbed with his despair that he had no appetite. In many instances, the "angels"—ordinary people whose lives radiate the love of Christ—come from the church. I know of no alternative to God's church as the ideal supporting community.

We must remember that Elijah's despair did not last forever, and his cause did not die out. Others have followed and have had their dark days and nights. One even went to the cross. And still, today, there are thousands who have not given up. They, along with their Lord, are able to strengthen and support us when we pass through dismal, discouraging times.

These words from the apostle Paul are inspirational, "We are afflicted in every way, but not crushed; perplexed, but not driven to despair; persecuted, but not forsaken; struck down, but not destroyed; always carrying in the body the death of Jesus, so that the life of Jesus may also be manifested in our bodies" (II Cor. 4:8–10). With that kind of trust in God, Paul had no danger of becoming depressed and discouraged.

The solution to Elijah's depression began with his "getting back to work." This is exactly what God called on him to do. God gave Elijah a task and sent him back to accomplish it. Like Elijah, we may sometimes need to get away from our lonely brooding and back into the work of sharing the burdens and responsibilities of others and of helping them to know the joys and rewards of following Christ.

Basically, the solution to depression involves trusting God. Without God and without Christ life inevitably becomes discouraging and dismal. There is no purpose for living. There is no hope for the future. In order for our lives to be lifted from despair we need to have a close and intimate relationship with God and the Lord Jesus Christ. God has work for us to do which will help us to feel that our lives are meaningful rather than useless. With Christ at our side, we need never despair.

6

"Can You Help Me Believe Again?"

Harold Hazelip

In the late seventeenth century John Bunyan wrote his famous allegory entitled *Pilgrim's Progress.* He tells the story of Christian's pilgrimage through the world in search of eternal life.

Christian stops by Interpreter's house and is not allowed to continue his journey before he visits a very dark room where a man sits in an iron cage. The man inside the cage sighs as if his heart will break. Christian says to him, "What art thou?" The man answers, "I am what I was not once." "But what art thou now?" asks Christian. "I am now a man of despair, and am shut up in it, as in this iron cage. I cannot get out." The man, once a Christian bound for the Celestial City, had gotten off the path and was hopelessly engulfed in the imprisonment of despair.

Perhaps you, too, have found yourself in a similar cage of despair and find it hard to believe as deeply as you once did.

Struggles of Faith

The despair of the caged man trapped by his own shaken faith has been shared by many. H. G. Wells, the British historian, once described God as "an ever-absent help in time of trouble." After studying history for fifty years, Wells concluded that "God does nothing, absolutely nothing at all in the affairs of earth."

A similar anguish is expressed in Psalm 73, which is designated as a psalm of Asaph. It tells the story of one man's struggle with his faith. It begins with the affirmation: "Truly God is good to the upright, to those who are pure in heart." While affirming God's goodness, he recalls a time when he was not sure—"But as for me, my feet had almost slipped; I had nearly lost my foothold" (v. 2, NIV). Having accepted the faith of his fathers, who believed that the righteous would prosper and the wicked would encounter hardships and perish, Asaph was puzzled by what he saw to the contrary. While he struggled, his wicked neighbors lived on the fat of the land. They were seemingly exempt from the sickness and the everyday burdens that plagued him and his family. They lived as though they were accountable to no one, not even God. Worse, they were full of pride and arrogant boasting. People fawned over them: "the people turn and praise them; and find no fault in them" (v. 10). Asaph concludes that the wicked are "always carefree, they increase in wealth" (v. 12, NIV).

The implied problem for faith is this: when such things happen, where is God?

But the good fortune of the wicked was not the only problem for Asaph. His devout pursuit of purity appears to have been in vain. Living a good and clean life has gotten him nowhere. So his soul becomes embittered and his heart burdened with grief; his faith begins to fail him.

Job's case was much the same. He was a man of absolute integrity before God, and yet he suffered grievous afflictions. He, too, questioned God's fairness because his integrity and moral purity had not brought the blessing and prosperity which he expected in return. For many, faith has become fragile, a "dimly burning wick." Its flame once burned brightly, but it has now become a dying ember.

Sources of Doubt

Some people have lost faith by the punishing struggle of life. With every plateau achieved the load gets heavier. No matter how hard they try, they lose. They become weary of trying, of fighting, of carrying the heavy responsibilities that life demands. They have been burned by life.

Some people have been disillusioned by broken trusts. People, ideas, things, the truth itself seem to have let them down. They don't know who or what to believe anymore. So they have become cynical and unwilling to trust.

Others have been burned by the flames of their emotions—emotions they don't understand and seem unable to control. They are plagued by fears or by feelings of hostility and depression. And they are unable to deal with those feelings.

A growing number of others have been burned by the church. Some people once believed so simply that God's people were all Christ-like. Then they discovered the distance between Christ and the behavior of many of his followers.

For whatever reason, these people's faith is on trial; it is a "dimly burning wick." Is there a solution? Can dimly burning wicks be blown into full flame again? Can those about to slip into despair regain their footing?

Wrong Expectations

C. S. Lewis, a notable twentieth-century convert to belief in Christ, was a bachelor in his mid-fifties when he married Joy Davidman. Three years after their marriage, Lewis watched his wife die of cancer. In *A Grief Observed*, written shortly after Joy's death, Lewis begins by telling how disappointed in God he was initially and how bitterly he charged God with the failure to live up to his promises.

However, by the end of the book, Lewis's perspective had changed: the problem lay in his own expectations of God and not in God's failure. He had predetermined what he thought God should do. He had expected God to perform according to his own illusions. When Lewis put aside these personal expectations and illusions, he was able to recognize what God had done. There had been many consolations and many evidences of God's intervention, although not at all in the forms he had anticipated. So, Lewis concluded, disillusionment is the child of illusion. Sometimes we reach the wrong conclusions because we begin with the wrong set of assumptions.

There was a time in history when Israel sat in a cage of despair and concluded that God had forsaken her. She complained, "My way is hidden from the LORD; my cause is disregarded by my God" (Isa. 40:27, NIV). She feared that God had forsaken her. To be sure, God had not performed according to Israel's expectations.

Help from Isaiah

Isaiah responds to Israel's despair by reminding her that God is everlasting, untiring, incredibly understanding, and that he gives strength to the weary and increases the power of the weak. To those who place confident hope in him, God proves himself to be an "ever-present help in time of trouble." His help may come in a variety of ways. It may come in the form of rescue or escape: "They who wait for the Lord . . . shall mount up with wings like eagles" (Isa. 40:31).

There may be times when God alters the shape of our lives. By his power we are delivered from our dilemmas and our circumstances are changed. As children we cried out for instant attention to our needs and perhaps we formed the habit of thinking that God, like a loving parent, would provide immediate relief and satisfy our every wish.

But we dare not presume that this is the only way God helps us. Isaiah speaks of running and not being weary (Isa. 40:31). Sometimes God enables us to solve our own problems, to use the power we possess to bring about change. We need to listen to Paul in Romans 8:28: "We know that in everything God works for good *with* those who love him" (italics mine). In everything, no matter what, God can work with us for good if we love him. He in no way promised to do it all, but assures us that he will work with us toward a constructive end if we love him.

According to Isaiah, there is yet another form of help. He describes it as the power to "walk and not faint" (Isa. 40:31). It is the gift of endurance. There are times when circumstances are not changed at all, but we are given the strength to live through them and be changed by them. Sometimes our only option is to stay with the struggle until it changes us for the better.

Help from the Psalms

Asaph can teach us something about recovering our faith and living with mystery. His first step toward recovery was his consciousness of the community of faith. He said, "If I had said, 'I will speak thus,' I would have been untrue to the generation of thy children" (Ps. 73:15). When he was tempted to throw his faith overboard, he shrank back in horror. Asaph could not bear to think of an entire generation growing up without ideals and living only for material values. The turning point was his sense of responsibility to the community of believers. Although unable to see God clearly, he could see the fellowship of believers. The community became a signpost pointing the way to God and restraining him from betrayal. He had said, "When I thought how to understand this [his faith dilemma], it seemed to me a wearisome task" (v. 16). As long as he remained isolated from the community of faith, there was no solution and no rest. It was all weariness—"until I went into the sanctuary of God" (v. 17).

Renewal increased dramatically when Asaph resumed participation in the worship of the community. He had been staying away from the sanctuary. His thoughts and energies had been centered on himself. But in the sanctuary he saw the people of God and was made to remember the story of God's dealings with them. In seeing God's people, he saw God.

A new perspective emerged for Asaph. He saw the prosperity of the wicked as a house of cards, vulnerable to the fickle winds of chance. "Then I understood their final destiny. Surely you place them on slippery ground; you cast them down to ruin" (vv. 17–18, NIV). Evil cannot stand the test of permanence.

This new assessment brings a strong assurance. God does not forsake his own. He is present in the valley and in the darkness. He offers comfort in distress, counsel for perplexity, and strength for weakness. Asaph declares, "My flesh and my heart may fail, but God is the strength of my heart. . . . I have made the Sovereign LORD my refuge . . ." (vv. 26, 28, NIV).

Help from Joseph's Example

The Old Testament story of Joseph offers some valuable assistance as well. The narrative of his life recorded in Genesis describes an amazing blend of positive and negative experiences. Joseph was the apple of his father's eye and was given preferential treatment. He was sheltered from the hard work required of his brothers. Furthermore, he was a dreamer and could interpret dreams. Some of his interpretations made him appear arrogant and he incurred the hostility of his brothers. Their resentment of him was so great that they began to plot his death. Circumstances came about, however, to prevent his being killed. Instead he was sold as a slave to a band of traders headed for Egypt. There he was sold to a man named Potiphar in whose household Joseph became a trusted overseer. But because of the malicious lies of Potiphar's wife, whose seductive advances Joseph had resisted, he was thrown into prison. Subsequently he was recruited by the pharaoh to be his grand vizier over all Egypt at a critical time in its history. Joseph experienced enough adversity and maltreatment in his life to plunge the strongest person into dark despair.

The impressive thing is the way in which Joseph dealt with the diverse calamities in his life. He could have responded with resentment, asking, "Why did this happen to me?" Instead, he seemed to ask, "What can I be thankful for and how can I use these experiences?" In every circumstance, Joseph found an occasion for gratitude. He employed the "strategy of gratitude" and it enabled him "in the worst of times to do the best of things."

None of us is free to determine the turn of events, but we are free to determine what response we will make to them. The choice is always ours. Therefore, the responsibility for the outcome lies with us, and we cannot pass the burden of that responsibility on to anyone else, including God.

Near the end of the biblical story of Joseph, his brothers became afraid that he would seek vengeance against them. But he wept and told them not to be afraid. Then he said, "As for you, you meant evil against me; but God meant it for good" (Gen. 50:20).

Our Response

Every believer can identify in some way with the man imprisoned in the cage of despair. Such times are inevitable. Under some circumstances it may seem that God has failed us and that we have trusted him in vain. Or we may feel exiled from his care and power. When these times come, faith may indeed become a dimly burning wick.

But listen to Isaiah as he assures the people of God whose faith had almost burned out, "Behold my servant, whom I uphold, my chosen, in whom my soul delights. . . . A bruised reed he will not break, and a dimly burning wick he will not quench" (Isa. 42:1–3). To all whose faith is but an ember, to all whose spiritual wick burns dim, take heart. Despair and resignation need not prevail. God has acted in your behalf. He has sent his Son, "the true light that enlightens every man," into the world (John 1:9). He can heal our bruises and fuel the flame of faith to make us brightly burning wicks.

Like Asaph, we can say:

> Whom have I in heaven but you?
> And being with you, I desire nothing on earth.
> My flesh and my heart may fail,
>   but God is the strength of my heart
>   and my portion forever [Ps. 73:25–26, NIV].

7
The Key to Self-Esteem

Joe R. Barnett

Charlie Brown, of "Peanuts" comic strip fame, is known as the classic loser. He pitches for the baseball team that never wins. When he represents his school in the spelling competition everyone knows how it will turn out, because Charlie Brown is a loser. It is no better socially. Charlie Brown keeps trying to earn the admiration and respect of others, but every attempt to be an achiever ends in disaster.

Yet we like Charlie Brown. I suspect his popularity comes from the fact that we see a bit of ourselves in this perennial loser. From our earliest days we are conditioned to believe the only way to be happy is to excel.

Recognition is reserved for the achievers. So, like Charlie Brown, we fantasize about rising to the top. But most of us remain in the category labeled "average."

What happens to all the Charlie Browns who face defeat after defeat? They grow up suffering with feelings of inferiority and insignificance. What they feel about *themselves* is largely determined by what *others* feel about them. If others consider them losers they grow up believing they are worthless.

Psychologists tell us one of our deepest needs is the need for self-esteem. How do we gain self-esteem?

It Hurts to Be a "Nobody"

Children can be incredibly cruel to each other. Do you remember the playground days when we chose sides to play ball? There were always some children who were chosen first. They were winners. Having them on the team gave a decided edge. And there were others who were always chosen last. They weren't wanted. They were a liability.

The same thing happened in the classroom. Some were winners; others were losers.

And it continues all through life. There is the housewife who spends her days tending to important family needs—and perhaps fantasizing about the glamorous roles of others. Ask her who she is, and she will likely tell you she is "just" a housewife. A society of distorted values has led her to believe she is "nobody."

There is the man who reaches middle age locked into a job that is going nowhere. To be "somebody" is to be climbing. But he stopped climbing long ago.

We measure people by their physical attractiveness, their athletic skills, their productivity, or their intelligence. Those who do not measure up are left to a life of frustration.

Guilt can also saddle us with feelings of inferiority. Charles Dickens's *Tale of Two Cities* has a character named Sydney Carton, whose life had been misspent. He'd had opportunities for achievement, but never had the self-discipline to do anything about them. He spent his life in London taverns, returning home each day in a drunken stupor.

The one thing which made Sydney Carton a man of destiny was his amazing resemblance to the hero of the story, Charles Darnay. At the climax of the book Charles Darnay was in prison in Paris awaiting execution. Sydney Carton arranged to visit Charles Darnay—and took his place in the prison cell. Carton, realizing his life had been wasted, seized this opportunity to make his life count for something. On the way to execution he said, "It is a far, far better thing I do, than I have ever done; it is a far, far better rest that I go to, than I have ever known." In his final act he wanted to make his wasted life useful.

Need for a Sense of Belonging

In *The Psychology of Self-Esteem*, Nathaniel Branden says our hunger for respect is so intense that we will stop at nothing to receive approval from others.

For example, the man who has no genuine self-esteem may suffer from the delusion of being a daring and shrewd speculator. He keeps losing money in one scheme after another—always blind to the fact that his plans are impractical. He may boast extravagantly. He thinks, "If only I could make it big they would admire and accept me."

A middle-aged woman's sense of personal value may depend on seeing herself as a glamorous, youthful beauty. Every facial wrinkle is a threat to her self-image. She may plunge into a series of romantic relationships, seeking acceptance. If we do not have self-esteem we may resort to shameful tactics to get others to acknowledge that we are someone special.

We desperately need a sense of belonging and acceptance. Nothing destroys our sense of worth so much as being ignored.

To overcome feelings of inferiority we need to know we are useful. We must feel our work makes a difference. Our self-image cannot tolerate the feeling of being a useless bystander in life.

Also, to overcome feelings of inferiority we need to have others to believe in us—to think we are valuable. Such persons have traditionally been found in families and among our friends. But the mobility of our society and the decline of family life have deprived many people of this one place where their value should be reaffirmed.

The film *Ordinary People* depicts a young man, from an

affluent family, who had become suicidal. In some ways he had everything going for him: he lived at the right address; his family was financially comfortable; he was a fine athlete. But he was miserable. One of the reasons was that his mother was distant and aloof. His attempts to become close to her failed. She was more concerned about her exciting life at the tennis courts than about her son. He was starving for her to say—in words or actions—"You are valuable to me."

Don't Give the Children's Bread to Dogs

Many people who came to Jesus were struggling with their self-esteem. Some, like the prostitute who washed Jesus' feet, came because their lives had been wasted. They were looking for someone who would tell them they were "somebody." There were sick people who wondered what terrible thing they had done to bring such suffering on themselves and their families. And there were people like Zacchaeus who were hated because of their profession.

All of these causes—a wasted life, guilt feelings, belonging to the wrong group—caused people to come to Jesus. They turned to him when their self-images were in shambles.

How do you overcome the nagging self-doubt which tells you your life is useless? Some people claim the answer is to simply and strongly affirm, "I am somebody!" Others say the answer is to assert yourself—"pull your own strings." But will these "positive thinking" methods really change the way we feel about ourselves?

The Gospels of Matthew and Mark (Matt. 15:21–28; Mark 7:24–30) tell about a woman who came to Jesus seeking help for her afflicted daughter. On the surface it sounds similar to many other Gospel stories, for most of them record the pleas of people who were hurting—the sick, the blind, and the crippled. But there is something especially poignant about this story. You see, this woman was a Syrophoenician. She was not born to the chosen people. This is the first recorded instance of a foreigner coming to Jesus for help.

Can you imagine how much courage it took for this woman to approach Jesus? She did not belong. She was constantly reminded that she was a "nobody."

What is remarkable about the Syrophoenician woman is her persistence. Immediately prior to her story is an account of some Pharisees who certainly weren't lacking in self-esteem. In fact, they thought so highly of themselves they wouldn't have come to Jesus for help. They belonged to the right group, they had not wasted their lives, and they were outwardly pure.

These Pharisees were a striking contrast to this woman who did not belong. When she approached Jesus he responded with what appears to be one of the coldest put-downs in the Bible: "Let the children first be fed, for it is not right to take the children's bread and throw it to the dogs" (Mark 7:27). The "children" were God's chosen people; the "dogs" were foreigners. Can you imagine how this must have made her feel? She was being reminded again that she did not belong.

Most people would respond to this rejection in anger, or by giving up. But not this woman. Her response is unforgettable: "Yes, Lord; yet even the dogs under the table eat the children's crumbs" (v. 28). She seemed to say, "Yes, perhaps I am a dog. I deserve nothing. But at least give me the crumbs." She displayed no arrogance, no bravado. She knew she was undeserving. But she won Jesus' heart. He said, "For this saying you may go your way; the demon has left your daughter" (v. 29).

The Key to Self-Esteem

This story is a miniature of the whole gospel. It offers the only real remedy for low self-esteem. All the modern remedies being offered to heal our sagging self-images overlook a crucial feature: we cannot create a sense of self-worth by our own thoughts and actions. No amount of self-assertion will make us feel good about ourselves. Nor can we remove our guilt or add to our stature merely by positive thinking.

The first step in achieving a sense of self-esteem is to recognize, as this woman did, that we are unworthy. We become somebody precisely at the point where we recognize that *God makes us somebody.*

God does not love us because we are valuable; we are valuable because God loves us. We are valuable because he created us in his own image. We are valuable because he died for us.

> Nothing in my hands I bring,
> Simply to thy cross I cling.

"While we were yet sinners Christ died for us" (Rom. 5:8). There is no "in" group and "out" group. He sees past our misspent years and our failures. He sees us for what we were meant to be. We are valuable to him.

Near the beginning of Paul's first letter to the Corinthians he makes this powerful and encouraging observation: "Not many of you were wise according to worldly standards, not many were powerful, not many were of noble birth" (I Cor. 1:26).

Paul was a good example of this. He was burdened with his past as a persecutor of Christians and he had a debilitating health problem. Tradition tells us his physical appearance was unimpressive. It's interesting that when God wanted his work done, he did not choose a great Athenian orator or athlete. He chose one who had reason to feel inferior. But God could use Paul's weakness to his glory. So Paul wrote, "I will all the more gladly boast of my weaknesses, that the power of Christ may rest upon me. . . . for when I am weak, then I am strong" (II Cor. 12:9–10).

Psychologists tell us unfulfilled desires for self-esteem lead to bitterness and frustration. Imagine the problems which are created in the child who constantly sits in front of a television set, absorbing the medium's standards for being somebody. To the girl it means beauty; to the boy it means being athletically gifted. Accepting these standards leads to frustration, because most people are rather ordinary.

There is an alternative. True self-esteem is found in Christ, who says, "You are accepted." In him life counts for something. You are valuable.

8
Win over Temptation

Joe R. Barnett

Otto von Bismarck, the European statesman, once walked into a room where he saw his picture on the wall. The picture showed a forceful man, as portraits of statesmen often do. "Is that the way I am supposed to look?" Bismarck asked. "That's not me." Pointing to another picture—one of Peter sinking beneath the waves—he said, "That's me!"

Most of us have responded similarly to the story of Peter's attempt to walk on water: "That's me." There are times when we are almost overwhelmed by life's struggles, as if they were huge waves threatening to engulf us.

Problems assault our faith. How can I trust God when life pummels me with tragedy? How can I believe in God when doubts keep gouging me? How can I keep my integrity in a world where integrity seems to pay no dividends?

This is the reason temptation is, in fact, temptation. It nibbles at us . . . gnaws at us . . . threatens to consume us. It returns again and again, refusing to take no for an answer.

News stories are about people who say yes to temptation: the politician who destroys his career by saying yes to the offered bribe; the husband who wrecks his marriage by saying yes to the temptation to be unfaithful; the athlete who ruins his future by saying yes to the bribe to "throw the game."

Such reports may leave the impression that no one can say no, but it is possible to win over temptation.

Temptation Is Not Reserved for Weaklings

Mark wrote about Jesus, "The Spirit immediately drove him out into the wilderness. And he was in the wilderness forty days, tempted by Satan" (Mark 1:12–13).

Just prior to this, Jesus had been baptized. It had been an impressive scene: the heavens had opened; the Spirit had descended; a voice had spoken from heaven. Surely nothing could block the fulfillment of Jesus' mission now. After this divine confirmation, surely he could not be tempted.

But Jesus was tempted! In fact, we have here the most detailed description of temptation to be found in the Bible. I'm glad we have this story. It gives us hope and courage. It was because he was one of us that he was tempted. He didn't sit in heaven shouting instructions from his throne. Rather he came to share our struggles—to be "tempted as we are" (Heb. 4:15).

Temptation is not reserved for derelicts and weaklings. It does not discriminate. It assaulted Jesus, whose life was in perfect submission to God.

Knowing his chosen disciples would face testing, Jesus taught them to pray, "Lead us not into temptation, but deliver us from evil" (Matt. 6:13). To them he said, "Temptations to sin are sure to come" (Luke 17:1). He warned Peter, "Simon, Simon, behold, Satan demanded to have you, that he might sift you like wheat" (Luke 22:31). And he knew some of his converts would fall away when temptation came (Luke 8:13).

Why did temptation come to Jesus at this particular moment? His baptism was the beginning of his public ministry. God had affirmed his mission with a voice from heaven. But not even the Son of God was to be immune from testing. What kind of son would he be? How would he use his power? Would he use it to dazzle the crowds for personal gain? Would he use it for his own advantage by turning stones into bread? Would he compromise his destiny by accepting an earthly reign?

Satan Attacks the Most Vulnerable Point

The specific temptations Jesus experienced are not our temptations. We are not tempted to turn stones into bread, or to jump from a tall building, or literally to bow before Satan. But the temptations Jesus faced, like ours, came at a vulnerable moment. Jesus' destiny was to serve others, and ultimately establish his kingdom by way of a cross. How painfully unappealing! Satan offered tempting short cuts. Jesus could bow to Satan and have his kingdom without the cross. He could satisfy his physical hunger by using his power to turn stones into bread.

Perhaps this was God's way of reminding us that temptation attacks each of us at our weakest point and most vulnerable moment. And perhaps this is why Paul warns new Christians, "Let not sin therefore reign in your mortal bodies, to make you obey their passions" (Rom. 6:12). Truly sin is like an alien power which reigns in a human life if it is permitted entrance. It is a wise—and strong—person who turns sin back at the temptation stage.

Temptation is shrewdly deceptive. It often comes when we think we are invulnerable. It came to Simon Peter when he was sure nothing could tempt him.

The apostle Paul once confronted those who took pride in their spiritual accomplishments, warning, "let any one who thinks that he stands take heed lest he fall" (I Cor. 10:12). Even the strongest person has his weak point, and Satan is persistent in finding it.

Temptation is certain to come. It comes to the student when he is tempted to violate honesty for the sake of a grade. It comes when we are tempted to deny our convictions to advance our careers. It comes when we ought to speak, but choose the expediency of remaining silent. It comes when it seems advantageous to lie rather than tell the truth. And it comes with unusual force when we see no gain in maintaining our integrity.

When Jesus turned away Satan's temptation we are told Satan went away. But he did not give up, for years later in Gethsemane Jesus struggled with the same kinds of questions he had faced in the desert. Would God's will prevail? Would he accept his destiny? Satan did not give up on *him*. And Satan will not give up on *us*.

"You Must Master It"

God confronted Cain after he had offered an unacceptable sacrifice. When Cain's anger surfaced, God said, "Why are you angry, and why has your countenance fallen? If you do well, will you not be accepted? And if you do not do well, sin is couching at the door; its desire is for you, but you must master it" (Gen. 4:6–7).

These words apply to us: Sin is couching at the door, and *we must master it*.

The names of those who fell under the temptations of Abscam have become household words. Public figures whose careers are destroyed by their failure to say no to temptation make good copy. Reporters don't win Pulitzer prizes for writing about those who refuse to compromise their convictions.

But there is another side which usually goes unreported: not everyone succumbs to these temptations. The cynic says, "Every man has his price." Not so! Jesus didn't. He was tempted in all points as we are, according to the author of Hebrews. And he adds, *"yet without sinning."* Jesus struggled with temptation in the desert, in Gethsemane, and at many points between. But he stood firm.

In Dostoevsky's *Brothers Karamazov*, there is a scene in which Jesus returned to medieval Spain during the Inquisition and visited those who claimed to speak in his name. They told him he made the wrong decision in the desert temptations. He should have accepted earthly power rather than suffering. He should have chosen physical bread and the acclaim of the crowds.

Imagine what it would have meant if Jesus had rejected his mission. But he didn't. He met and defeated the tempter.

Jesus, the Ultimate Defense

The message is clear: we don't have to suffer defeat either. We will be tested, and we may at times stumble and fall. Like Simon Peter, we may fail Jesus when the test comes. But, also like Peter, we do not have to accept that failure as final.

Remember Jesus' words to Peter? Jesus told Peter that Satan wanted to sift him like wheat. But then he added, "I have prayed for you that your faith may not fail" (Luke 22:32). We do not stand alone in our "hour of trial." He stands with us. We are not helpless against Satan's temptations, for we have the ultimate defense—the presence of Christ.

There is encouragement in Paul's letter to the Corinthians. When he warned about the dangers and temptations facing them, he added the promise: "No temptation has overtaken you that is not common to man. God is faithful, and he will not let you be tempted beyond your strength, but with the temptation will also provide the way of escape, that you may be able to endure it" (I Cor. 10:13).

We may feel the full force of Satan's power; may be tempted to believe there is no future in maintaining our integrity; may, at times, feel we are sinking. But we will not be defeated if we will remember that Jesus stands with us—and "he who is in you is greater than he who is in the world" (I John 4:4).

Leaning on this assurance, many people have successfully met their time of testing.

There was Joseph, who, when he was tempted by Potiphar's wife to enter an adulterous relationship, courageously said, "No!"

There were those brave Christians of the first few generations of Christianity who were told they must confess, "Caesar is Lord." Their time of testing came when they were called before magistrates and were asked if they were Christians. It came when they were told they could go home to their families in freedom if they would only offer a "meaningless" sacrifice to a pagan god.

There have been those in our own century who have lived under totalitarian regimes which felt threatened by those with Christian commitments. There is always the temptation to bend, to compromise. Many Christians have successfully met such testing—some at the cost of their lives. There must be an act of the will which refuses to compromise. If necessary a Christian will accept being bypassed for a deserved and desired promotion; he will accept indignities with courage. Admirable will power was exercised by those early Christians as they were denied the common privileges open to others. They survived by an act of will.

Yet we cannot fight temptation alone. It is God who "delivers us from evil." We have a faithful high priest who pleads our cause and intercedes for us. God has promised he will not allow us to be tempted beyond our capacity.

Temptation is unavoidable, but failure is not. Because Jesus won the victory we can, too.

9

The Fractured Family

Harold Hazelip

A comic strip called "Peanuts," born in the 1950s, quickly became an American institution. Charlie Brown, Lucy, and Linus captured our hearts. We loved Snoopy's fantasy world, Linus's insecurity, and Charlie Brown's anxiety. We found their grown-up conversation amusing. The "Peanuts" characters became the subject of a Broadway play and countless seasonal television specials. Charlie Brown may have the most recognized face in the Western world.

Charlie Brown and Lucy may be known throughout the world, but their families certainly are not. I feel that I have known these children for more than twenty years, but I have never seen their parents. Nor have I seen the parents of their friends. "Peanuts" is a world without adults.

The humor of "Peanuts" is in the fact that the parents are missing. Charles Schulz has portrayed an unreal world of missing parents, and the scenes are funny in the world of "Peanuts." But in real life the world of absentee parents is not so funny.

Do you recall those spot announcements which asked: "Parents, do you know where your children are?" Another question is equally important: "Children, do you know where your parents are?"

What difference does it make in the growth and development of the child if *both* parents are present?

A Society Without Parents

The scientific evidence is overwhelming: Children who grow up interacting with both parents have the ideal situation for attaining good emotional development. As Professor Armand Nicholi said, "What has been shown to contribute most to the emotional development of the child is a close, warm, sustained, and continuous relationship with *both* parents."

In studies conducted at the Children's Hospital Medical Center in Boston, observers noticed the pattern of relationships that developed between infant and parents. Researchers noted that, as early as four weeks, it is obvious that the infant is able to differentiate between mother, father, and stranger. Observers noticed also that the two parents played with their children in different ways, held them in different ways, and established different modes of interacting with the child. An important lesson came out of this research: a mother and father do not duplicate one another's contributions to the development of the child; they complement each other. Mother and father work as a partnership, with each supplying something necessary for the development of the child.

I am impressed that the contribution of both parents is so significant that it can be measured when the child is only a few weeks old. If this is true, it makes one wonder about the importance of both parents at age three, six, ten, or sixteen. Each parent is necessary in the development of the child at every point.

According to a study by the World Health Organization,

"What is believed to be essential for mental health is that the infant and young child should experience a warm, intimate, and continuous relationship with his mother." Then the group presented evidence that many psychoneuroses and character disorders can be attributed to the mother's absence. In the years following that statement, research throughout the world has demonstrated that even a brief separation from the mother can profoundly affect the child's physical and emotional development. The same is true of the child without a father.

The presence of both parents throughout our development is the vital factor in teaching us our own sexual identity and how to react to the opposite sex. A boy who grows up with his father nearby learns what it means to be a man. He may learn, from watching the relationship between the parents, how a man responds to his wife. A girl learns, from having both parents nearby, how to deal with the opposite sex. Studies have shown that girls who have been deprived of their fathers tend to become uncertain in the presence of males. Some girls retreat, not knowing how to respond in the presence of males. Some girls become overly aggressive, trying to prove their worth to the opposite sex.

Dr. Donald M. Joy, in a lecture about the development of the child's conscience, suggested that there is no better illustration of the effects of the absent parent than Fonzie of the television series "Happy Days." We do not know anything about Fonzie's parents. They are absent. Fonzie lives by himself in a little apartment behind the Cunninghams' house. He has, according to Dr. Joy, the typical characteristics of the child with the absent father. He has an exaggerated sense of masculinity which causes him to play two roles: the "ladies' man" and the "enforcer." In the absence of his parents, he has taken on a distorted picture of his identity and his relationship to others.

Fonzie is funny on the television screen, but he is not a

well-integrated personality. By the time Fonzie is twenty-five or thirty years old, he may not be funny anymore. He is hardly prepared to take on a responsible role. His distorted ideas will not give him the identity for becoming a good husband and father.

A number of studies have shown the results when children grow up without one or both parents. One study, published in the *Archives of General Psychiatry*, analyzed the effect the periodic absence of the father had on two hundred children, aged three to eighteen, when the absence was due to the father's military occupation. Researchers found that the children's reaction to the father's absence involved a rageful protest over the desertion, irrational guilt and a need for punishment, fear of being abandoned, and a loss of control over the impulses.

Surely there are exceptions to this general pattern. Many young people cope with life quite well after losing a parent through desertion or death. But no one would seriously claim that it makes no difference. Several studies have shown that the loss of a father contributes to the child's low motivation for achievement, low self-esteem, susceptibility to group influence, and susceptibility to delinquency.

Why Parents Are "Missing"

Of course, there are times when the absence of a parent is unavoidable, but this absence is never desirable. What concerns us are those absences which are avoidable—and the majority of them are! More than a million children each year are involved in divorce cases. Thirteen million children under age eighteen are without one or both parents. These children are often the victims of our own lack of consideration and self-centeredness. Divorce becomes the answer to the desire for self-fulfillment. But one person's self-fulfillment may be the other person's destruction.

It is not divorce alone which results in absentee parents. With our high standard of living, we demand two incomes. Today more than fifty percent of the mothers with preschool children work outside the home. Nearly six million preschool children have working mothers. To be sure, there are instances where the child is taken care of by someone who provides warmth and affection. But in other cases, the child is in the care of institutions which can provide none of the warmth that the child demands.

Dr. Joy also commented, "For all practical purposes, many American fathers, by their work practices and their perceptions about what a father's responsibilities are might as well be dead or divorced, because they're actually not functioning with their children." The average American father, Dr. Joy tells us, spends only twenty minutes per day in the same room with his child. And when researchers implanted microphones in the infant's clothing to record verbal interaction, the average amount of time a father spends with a preschool child is thirty-eight seconds per day. Cross-cultural studies show that parents in the United States spend less time with their children than parents in almost any country in the world.

It has been said that we have become a father-absent society. Part of this is caused by the fact that many of us live in cities where fathers must commute great distances to work and back, leaving little time each day for the father to be at home during the child's waking hours. In an earlier time fathers worked near the home, and the children could see him at his work.

But there is another reason why fathers are often absent. We are absorbed in our own self-fulfillment. The limited time at home is an occasion to catch up on our hobbies, which exclude the children. Children are an obstacle to our enjoyment of our friends or hobbies.

The comments of a perceptive eight-year-old who was asked, "What is a grandmother?" emphasize this point:

> A grandmother is a lady who has no little children of her own. She likes other people's. A grandfather is a man grandmother.
>
> Grandmothers don't have to do anything except be there. They are old so they shouldn't play hard or run. It is enough if they drive us to the market and have a lot of dimes ready. When they take us for walks, they slow down past things like pretty leaves and caterpillars. They never say "Hurry up."
>
> Usually grandmothers are fat, but not too fat to tie your shoes. They wear glasses and funny underwear. They can take their teeth and gums out. Grandmothers don't have to be smart, only answer questions like "Why isn't God married?" and "How come dogs chase cats?" When they read to us they don't skip or mind if we ask for the same story over again.
>
> Everybody should try to have a grandmother, especially if they don't have television, because they are the only grownups who have time.

Every child needs to grow up in an atmosphere where both mother and father have the time to answer trivial questions, take walks, and play games. Many children have everything but the presence of both parents.

There is an additional concern which must be mentioned. What will happen to a society which neglects its children? What will be the result when an entire generation has been educated only by television and the peer group? There is something wrong in a society where children between the ages of six and sixteen see both parents less than twenty minutes per day and watch television four to five hours each day.

A whole set of forces is working together to pull families apart. And when families are fractured, so also is the fabric which holds a society together. Families are being fractured by the values of our culture. If our highest values are the increase in our living standard and the fulfillment of our selves, the time spent in any other activity—especially in looking after someone else—may seem to be a nuisance. If the family is to be brought together again, we need nothing less than a new set of values.

This will not be easy. I believe the first step in discovering a new set of values is to rediscover an old story. The faith which Christians share is about the One who gave himself up for others. "Scarcely for a righteous man will one die. . . . But God commendeth his love toward us, in that, while we were yet sinners, Christ died for us" (Rom. 5:7–8, KJV). This truth is repeated many times in the Bible, and it is stated in many different ways.

As you read the story of Jesus, one of the first discoveries you make is that his life challenged the values of his day. He had time for little children who were brought to him. He had time for poor people, sick people, and others whose lives might have interfered with his self-fulfillment. In fact, he challenged the values of his day so much that his life ended on a cross—in his dying for others.

Jesus' life, death, and resurrection changed lives and formed a community of believers who tried to live as he had lived. No one could follow Jesus without changing his values and living with a new attitude toward others. Paul put it this way: "Let each of you look not only to his own interests, but also to the interests of others. Have this mind among yourselves, which you have in Christ Jesus" (Phil. 2:4–5).

The Church Helps

Jesus' story had an impact on communities of people who now learned to live with one another. Jesus' story also had an impact on families. On several occasions the writers of the New Testament give instructions to families. "Husbands, love your wives," Paul says, or, "Wives, be subject to your husbands" (Eph. 5:21–25). "Children, obey your parents," or, "Fathers, do not provoke your children" (Eph.

6:1–4). What is striking about these instructions is the conviction that Jesus Christ had made an impact on family life. Husbands and wives found a new meaning to words like "love" and "submission." The story of Christ put an end to the drive for self-fulfillment. Christian families found the resource for committing themselves to others.

This is the resource we need today. The other person is made "in the image of God" and is one "for whom Christ died" (Gen. 1:27; Rom. 14:15). When you hear the story of Jesus Christ, you discover a new way of looking at others—their needs, their anxieties, and especially their value. Undoubtedly our absence and our thoughtlessness—our inability to respond to silly questions and play childish games—results from our inability to take others seriously. Christ has taught us to take others seriously.

The Christian life was, for the early Christians, a family matter. The regular worship services were often conducted in the familiar atmosphere of homes. The congregation might have consisted of only a few families. Christians practiced their faith in family units (Rom. 16:5–15). The church provided a support system for struggling families.

One of the factors making an impact on family life today is the extraordinary mobility of our society. We move to new towns where we have no network of relationships. Because we may be moving again soon, we resign ourselves to not making new contacts. The family that is alone in the city, cut off from the moral support that relatives once provided, is denied an important resource for struggling through a crisis. We have no others who are deeply concerned for our survival.

What we notice in the early church is that the Christian family was a part of a community that cared for its members. The church supported the families in maintaining their unique values, showing others that they were not alone with their convictions. The church today provides us with support for holding our families together.

Someone has said that Jesus Christ has liberated us from "excessive self-concern." This may be the one value which can also liberate families from the forces which pull them apart. We do not have to neglect or ignore others. We can regard them as ones "for whom Christ died."

"When anyone is united to Christ, there is a new world" (II Cor. 5:17, NEB). We can also have a new kind of family.

10
Before Divorce

Harold Hazelip

Ingmar Bergman's *Scenes from a Marriage* has to be one of the most depressing films ever made. The film was first shown in the mid-1970s, and is a collection of segments from a series which appeared on Swedish television and later on American television.

In the movie, an affluent couple in early middle age seem, at first glance, to have an ideal marriage. A quick look at their home indicates that they have no economic difficulties. In the opening scene they look like the ideal family as they sit before a photographer.

But soon we witness a series of scenes portraying the disintegration of a marriage. To the outside world they are the perfect couple, but they live in mutual torment. They humiliate each other. They argue about the in-laws. They have perfect memories when it comes to recalling the hurts and pain each received from the other over the years. They exploit every weakness discovered in one another during two decades of marriage. They know how to hurt one another as no one else could.

Finally divorce comes. But they cannot walk away from this intimate bond after twenty years as if nothing had happened. The divorce simply leads to more pain.

It is a familiar theme—the disintegration of a home. *Who's Afraid of Virginia Woolf?* is a play which vividly depicts the capacity of two people to turn their marriage into mutual torture. I suspect that these stories—like most fiction—are being enacted in real life. In fact, behind every divorce there is a story of disappointment and tragedy.

How does a marriage come to this? Ask any new couple, and they will tell you that their marriage was "made in heaven." They could not bear to destroy each other as George and Martha do in *Who's Afraid of Virginia Woolf?*

But about one in three of these happy couples experiences failure. How do you explain this? Perhaps if we knew what caused this disintegration, we could do something about it.

Trials of Intimacy

Some people claim that the marriage relationship, by its very nature, leads to failure. Imagine the annoyances that can accumulate when two people live under the same roof: the toothpaste tube is squeezed rather than rolled. More seriously, there are the in-law problems, the jealousies, the neglect, or the harsh words.

Where does the disintegration begin in a relationship that fails? Two well-known marriage counselors, William Lederer and Don Jackson, in *Mirages of Marriage*, say that the failure begins during the honeymoon. While they are dating, both people constantly attempt to be as attractive as possible. The man is bored by opera, but he buys tickets for an opening night, puts on uncomfortable clothes, and spends more money than he can afford because of what she wants. She is a city girl who dislikes walking two or three blocks to the bus. But if she is in love, she may get up before sunrise and go fishing with him—even though the sight of a flopping fish may disgust her.

Things change after the wedding. We might have thought during the courtship that we had no differences. But marriage reveals that we are very different. We notice annoying habits that we never saw before. He tells the same stories over and over. She leaves the kitchen a mess at night.

Lederer and Jackson conclude from interviews with normal families that the disintegration process in a marriage is usually triggered by what husband and wife *neglect* to say and do. No one intends to destroy a relationship. Neglect and thoughtlessness result in failures to live up to the spouse's expectations.

What kind of neglect destroys a relationship? First, husbands and wives may fail to agree on their areas of responsibility. This can be particularly hurtful at the beginning of a marriage. What would a relationship be like if each little responsibility has to be specially assigned? Who prepares the budget? Who waxes the floor? And when the children are born, whose responsibility is the chauffering or the PTA?

In many instances our culture has passed on a tradition of "women's roles" and "men's roles." We may assume that men do the outside work and women work inside the house. If doing the work at home is reduced to a power struggle, and if each partner is afraid of demeaning himself or herself by doing the unpleasant work of the house, marriage may begin to disintegrate. The fact is that the garbage needs to be taken out, the baby's diapers have to be changed, and other less-than-exciting chores must be done. It may sound unromantic for the husband and wife to assign authority and responsibility, as if marriage were a system governed by rules. But genuine love can flourish better in a relationship where there is order than in one where there is chaos.

I mentioned earlier the shock that comes to many young couples when each recognizes that this other person is different—with different parents, different upbringing, and different habits. The awakening comes very early in the marriage, and it must be dealt with if the marriage is to grow. Marriages frequently fail when two people do not understand their differences are only differences, rather than marks of inferiority.

I have watched American tourists overseas complain about the food because Europeans or others do not prepare their meals as we do. We fall into the same trap in our marriage relationships. Her ignorance about sports is a sign of a poor upbringing. His tastes in entertainment and food show his inferiority. Once these negative value judgments begin, misunderstanding grows and grows. These criticisms are a disparagement of her family or an insult to his intelligence. We may disguise the barbs as wit. But the impression comes through, "You are inferior! You are inferior!"

One of the biggest challenges of a young marriage is to face these differences in a positive way. All differences are not evidence of inferiority, but some are signs of weakness. Once you are married, you may recognize weaknesses in the other person you never saw before. And your companion will recognize your weaknesses, too. Some of them may be serious. They may threaten your relationship. The Christian has an important insight into this problem. This is the way it is with God's relationship with his people. The heart of the gospel is that God loved us "while we were yet sinners." He did not love us because we were particularly lovable, or because we had a right to his love. He loved us in spite of our weaknesses and our character flaws. He showed us that, in Jesus Christ, we can change.

Growing Through Crises

The popular idea about love suggests that we love those who attract us and stop loving those whose blemishes we come to see. But the Christian has learned what love is. In marriage, too, "love suffers long and is kind" (I Cor. 13:4, NKJV). Love looks beyond weaknesses to the real person behind them.

Once the honeymoon is over, we may begin to take the

other person for granted, to stop being concerned about his or her wishes, or to look for weaknesses we never saw before. But some marriages become very strong. How do such couples avoid these pitfalls? One answer, I think, is to go on wooing as we did before the wedding. John Updike once commented, "Courting a wife takes tenfold the strength of winning an ignorant girl." We probably fail because we refuse to make the effort. Those acts of love that meant so much before the wedding—the flowers, the gifts, the compliments—are likely to have the same effect after the wedding. They communicate to us that we are special.

Marriage is like a living organism. It is always in the process of growth and change. It can be in good or bad health. It can flourish or die through the years.

We are familiar with crises that a child passes through as he develops into a mature adult. There is the adjustment in the first few years when the child learns the basic skills of playing in a group and living with others. There is the crisis of adolescence, often marked by rebellion. There is a crisis in middle age. A number of marriage counselors have suggested that marriage has its own crises which demand special attention if the marriage is to remain healthy. Dr. Bernard Harnik, the Swiss marriage counselor, observed that divorce is most frequent in the fourth-to-fifth year of marriage and in the sixteenth-to-eighteenth year.

In the first crisis period, it becomes obvious that the honeymoon is over. The young professional becomes more and more absorbed in his work. Conversation may die out. Each partner accuses the other, "You don't love me anymore." They feel they do not understand each other, and probably never did understand each other. Dr. Harnik tells about a young woman who fell in love with a neighbor and then asserted that she had never loved her husband. She was astonished to see the love letters she had written in the first few months of their marriage. Fortunately, this couple resolved the crisis.

The second crisis in marriage may be associated with the psychological changes that come with middle age. A frequent theme in movies is the middle-aged man who has always been a model husband and father, but now becomes unfaithful to his wife. He may want to prove his youthfulness at the moment of his inner anxiety about growing older. His wife has her own fears about this period of her life. They may feel that their marriage has become an empty routine.

Crises may be inevitable in a marriage. Marriage is a complicated interweaving of two lives. But a crisis can be an occasion for growth, an opportunity for the two to take an inventory of their relationship. The middle-aged couple may recognize that the preoccupations of the years—the children, their professions—have drawn them apart. They may recognize how much they need each other. In moments of personal anxiety, no one can reassure a person of his worth in the same way that a husband or wife can.

Several years ago Abigail Van Buren was asked, "How does a woman make a good marriage great?" She answered, "That's easy. She simply works like a dog." Good marriages don't come by accident. They require the conscientious efforts of two dedicated people. But the results can be well worth the effort. David and Vera Mace, who are both marriage counselors, conclude from their forty years of marriage that marriage can be the most satisfying experience of all. Winston Churchill said it well: "Marriage is the best thing I ever did."

God's Gift

In *We Can Have Better Marriages If We Really Want Them*, David and Vera Mace suggest that if we had never heard of marriage and it were being suggested to us for the first time, we would probably respond that marriage is a wonderful idea. It meets so many of our fundamental needs. We would want to establish marriage if this had not already been done.

This is the message of Genesis. "It is not good for the man to be alone," God said at the very beginning (Gen. 2:18, NEB). The man was incomplete without that special person with whom he could share an intimate relationship. When God created a partner for him, Adam virtually broke out singing: "This is now bone of my bones and flesh of my flesh; she shall be called 'woman,' for she was taken out of man" (Gen. 2:23, NIV).

Eve was so much like Adam, and yet so different. The Bible's point is clear: Man and woman are meant to share this intimate relationship. "For this reason a man will leave his father and mother and be united to his wife, and they will become one flesh" (Gen. 2:24, NIV). No relationship is like this.

Jesus made a powerful comment on this text when he was asked if divorce is lawful. He answered, "what God has joined together, let man not separate" (Matt. 19:6, NIV). It is God who joins two people together in marriage.

I described some of the possibilities for anger and hostility when two people live in the closeness of marriage. But there are also infinite possibilities in having someone say publicly, "I will love you, no matter what." When these vows are taken seriously, there is one person with whom I can be totally vulnerable. One person will love me when I am ill, old, injured, or destitute. In fact, I have made the same promise. There is enormous risk in a lifelong promise, but such a promise makes possible a relationship that cannot be compared to any other.

There are people who experiment with sexual relationships outside of marriage. These people may explain that they are "keeping their options open." This may sound like freedom. But God has placed sexual intimacy within the context of marriage, of lifelong commitment. Sexual intimacy without marriage not only goes against God's will, but it also does not allow trust and true oneness to exist.

Divorce is a refusal to accept the intimacy God has provided. This is why Jesus said, "what God has joined together, let man not separate." Divorce is like splitting an organism apart; it is a terrible amputation. It involves taking apart the very thing which God has united.

In the Old Testament, God is compared to a husband by the prophets Hosea, Isaiah, and Jeremiah. Israel, his bride, had failed him and defiled his name. If ever a husband had grounds for separation, God did. On one occasion, the people surmised that he had divorced his faithless wife. God replied, "Where is your mother's certificate of divorce with which I sent her away?" (Isa. 50:1, NIV). He was the husband whose love would never let go. He would not accept defeat. He repeatedly took her back. Without his forgiveness, God's marriage with Israel would have ended in divorce.

The early Christians who knew Christ as the faithful bridegroom of the church learned something about their own marriages. Love has a meaning for the Christian that may be incomprehensible to those who talk only about romantic love. Love involves forgiveness, kindness, and placing the interests of the other before one's own.

A Work of Art

Someone has said that marriage is a work of art that is never finished. It is the most challenging and complex of all the works a human being can create. It is not like painting, poetry, architecture, or a novel. We can never put down the tools of this art form, step back, and pronounce the work complete. Marriage is an ongoing project.

Unlike most of our artistic works, marriage involves intense cooperation between two people. Husband and wife bring to their marriage their personal histories, their bodies, their talents, their fears, their dreams, their infirmities—all that makes them distinct from every other person living. They are unique as persons. But they believe that with each other they can have a fuller life than either could know alone.

Can this uniting of two lives work? I know about the propaganda against this promise, "for better for worse." But I also know about any number of good marriages. And those relationships cannot be compared to the provisional relationships in which people refuse to commit themselves.

Good marriages will have their share of misunderstandings, personal and financial crises, and disagreements. But, as Clayton Barbeau suggests, if the quality of the marriage relationship is good and our mutual commitment to our relationship unquestioned, then the problems we confront—even our disagreements with one another—can become sources of a deeper love. To truly love one another is to accept the other person in his or her differences from oneself, to strive to understand the other's point of view, to forgive the other's failures in the relationship, and to seek the other's good ahead of one's own self-seeking.

11
Mid-life Crisis

Joe R. Barnett

We can anticipate with considerable accuracy every stage in the development of a child. Parents who never had parenting experience take comfort in the fact that Dr. Spock has prepared them for every possible crisis in their child's life. He has told them how to confront the various childhood diseases, how to meet the challenge of the "terrible twos," and how to deal with each crisis which comes.

Experts also have carefully documented the predictable crises associated with adolescence—the bewilderment, the rebellion, the confusion.

Nor do the crises stop here. Our entire lives are composed of critical moments in which we either grow or regress.

Gail Sheehy, in *Passages*, writes, "We are not unlike a particularly hardy crustacean. The lobster grows by developing and shedding a series of hard, protective shells. Each time it expands from within, the confining shell must be sloughed off. It is left exposed and vulnerable until, in time, a new covering grows to replace the old."

We have plotted every stage of growth in the child from infancy through adolescence. But, as Sheehy asks, "Where are the guidelines on how to get through the Trying Twenties and the Forlorn Forties?"

Unfortunately, we are not so informed about these years. Yet the crises are real.

The Need to Keep Jumping Hurdles

A short story by John Cheever, "O Youth and Beauty," details a routine which occurred at the end of every Saturday night party in Shady Hill. In the early morning hours, after everyone had lost track of time, Trace Bearden would begin chiding Cash Bentley about his advancing age and thinning hair. Soon Cash would take his position, and Trace would raise his revolver to fire through an open window. Then Cash would be off and running—over the sofa, the tables, the fire screen, and woodbox. It was amazing to see this forty-year-old man clear the obstacles so gracefully.

Cash, a former track star, took pride in the fact that he could still hurdle the furniture. Then one evening, after the usual chiding, Cash went through the routine again. This time the old hurdler failed to clear the sofa and ended up with a broken leg.

After that life was never the same. The pain and inconvenience were bad enough. But there was something much worse. Cash could not accept the fact that he had failed. He became depressed and miserable. The one thing he had always taken pride in—his youthful athletic ability—was fading. No one ever encouraged him to hurdle the furniture again. He was hurt by the change in others' perception of him. Worst of all, there was a change in the way Cash thought of himself. His self-esteem was shattered.

We are, as Anne Morrow Lindbergh wrote in *A Gift from the Sea*, a society which overemphasizes youth, action, and material success, and "belittles the afternoon of life." Our overemphasis on youth and physical prowess carries the seeds of severe emotional crisis. If a man's self-esteem is derived from his capacity to clear the hurdles with grace and speed, his sense of personal worth is sure to decline with increasing age. We don't like being reminded that we're getting older. It's threatening to us when the doctor says, "A man of your age should. . . ." When you're told that you are "holding your age well," you're not sure you have received a compliment.

Someone has said, "What we are up against is a social conspiracy to make youth last a lifetime." The commercials exhorting us to "cover up" the gray hair and the wrinkles suggest that our value lies in our remaining youthful. The woman who has been conditioned all her life to believe that her worth is found in being alluring and charming—and that the only way to have these qualities is to retain her youthfulness—doesn't easily accept the thought of becoming a grandmother.

For many people, middle age is connected with losing something desirable that will never return. A man may realize that his teen-age son is now his equal in strength and athletic ability. For a woman, the appearance of wrinkles may tell her she has reached an undesirable stage of life.

The temptation, of course, is to prove you haven't lost anything. Movies frequently depict the middle-aged man who, after years as a model husband and father, surprisingly ruptures these relationships, trying to prove his youthfulness by a series of romantic flings.

But we can't deny the inevitable. As Cash Bentley learned, nature has a way of forcing us to accept the reality of this new stage of life.

Looking at the Balance Sheet

There is another kind of crisis that we can't ignore at mid-life. In *Games People Play*, Eric Berne describes the reevaluation which takes place with the coming of middle age. He calls it the "Balance Sheet." You look at the balance sheet of your life and ask, "Am I on schedule with what I wanted to do with my life?" You look at your career, recognizing you're probably as effective as you will ever be. You are likely at the height of your potential, having spent most of your adult years getting where you are now. For years you have been "on the way." Now, in a sense, you have "arrived." This realization may be good news or bad news—but it can't be avoided.

How do you cope with this change in your life? As Gail Sheehy asks, "Is there life after youth?"

Every stage of life has its crises. But a crisis is not a catastrophe; it is a turning point, a challenge to be met. If we successfully meet it, the crisis leads to a richer, more meaningful life.

As we come to mid-life we face inevitable decline in physical capacities. Some people stumble over the negative side of this reality and view the rest of their lives as a sure and unwelcome decline.

But there is another side to it—this can be the most fulfilling time of life, the time for which we have been preparing throughout our youth. It is no cliche to say that middle age is the prime of life, for the world is, in fact, largely run by those who are middle-aged.

Granted, youths set the sports records, but those in middle age make the important decisions that most affect our lives. We do not trust these decisions to the inexperienced. Those who are given the decisionmaking responsibilities of corporate and public service are, in the main, middle-aged. Someone has observed that the one-fifth of the population between forty and sixty is obliged to carry the world for the other four-fifths.

Thousands of middle-aged people regard this as the turning point in their lives, the moment for which they have prepared all through life. They turn from the trivial values of physical strength and beauty to the responsibilities of leadership.

It is the middle-aged who make the important decisions in the church. It is not without reason that these decisions have been placed in the hands of those known as elders and not novices. They also make the decisions in government. We usually consider the coming of middle age as only the beginning of one's qualifications for responsible political positions.

"Buying Up the Time"

Barbara Fried, in *The Middle-Age Crisis*, argues that it's a matter of attitude. "As long as the middlescent concentrates on what used to be—that is, on the disagreeable fact that strength, sexual vigor, activity, youthful beauty, stamina and potential are waning—he (or she) will never be able to accept the idea that experience, assurance, substance, skill, achievement, wisdom, success, the judgment to see what is truly important more than compensate for the loss of youthful power."

So the first step in meeting the mid-life challenge is to recognize the falsity of the notion that our value is measured by youthfulness.

A phrase in the New Testament describes the attitude which will cause us to successfully meet the challenge of the mid-life stage. Paul speaks of "buying up the time" (Eph. 5:16; Col. 4:5, AB).

If middle age is the time when we begin looking at the balance sheet, asking what we have achieved, the idea of "buying up the time" is particularly appropriate.

In our late teens and early twenties we felt there was plenty of time to achieve our life's goals. But when we reach thirty-five or forty we begin to realize how time flies. We become aware that wasted years can't be retrieved. We begin to wonder how important the things are in which we are investing our time. What legacies are we leaving behind? Are we doing anything more important than leaping hurdles in our fortieth year, pretending we're still in our youth?

The problem is that many of us reach middle age without a program for the next stage of life. Worship at the altar of youth and beauty will not serve us any longer. If there are no goals to help us meet the challenges of middle age we will be frustrated. If we have not established such goals we are likely to try one of those silly escapes to prove our manhood or desirability.

The Trivial Versus the Important

Carl Jung, the psychologist, says what we need in mid-life is to know life more deeply, to know our ultimate destiny to fulfill. Most of all, he says, we need to find a religious outlook on life.

There is abundant evidence that those who have met these years with a religious program have found life filled with meaning. Look, for example, at Paul, the most eloquent spokesman for early Christianity and the writer of a major portion of the New Testament. As he wrote to the Philippians he was on trial for his life. In the midst of this crisis he wrote, "Not that I have already obtained this or am already perfect; but I press on to make it my own, because Christ Jesus has made me his own. . . . one thing I do, forgetting what lies behind and straining forward to what lies ahead, I press on toward the goal for the prize of the upward call of God in Christ Jesus" (Phil. 3:12–14).

Paul did not look back to an irretrievable past with regret, nor to the future as a time of inevitable decline. Facing advancing years—and possible execution—he still spoke of goals to be pursued.

Many people fail to conquer the mid-life crisis because, like Cash Bentley, they continue hanging on to the trivial. At mid-life we must pursue the important, not the trivial; the lasting, not the mundane. This time of life can be a catastrophe if we refuse to focus on the important goals. But if we find important, spiritual goals it can be a time of exciting, meaningful growth.

We have needed the struggles of growing up, the creative discoveries and disciplines of every age. But at mid-life we see clearly that they have only been to prepare us for the greater challenges of continued growth in later years.

If we properly handle the challenges we can say with Robert Browning's Rabbi Ben Ezra:

> Grow old along with me!
> The best is yet to be,
> The last of life, for which the first was made.

12

Coping with Illness

Batsell Barrett Baxter

At any given time there is a generous cross section of the American people who are ill. Some are shut-ins who are permanently ill and are confined to their homes, to rest homes, or to sanitariums. Others are in hospitals on a relatively temporary basis. Still others are confined to their homes by some simple, relatively brief illness. Then there are others who are not ill, but who have physical handicaps as they do their daily tasks. On any given day in any given year there are several million people across the land who are ill and who are temporarily or permanently deprived of participating in many of the normal activities of life.

Because of my own experiences, I feel a special closeness to others who are ill. Since March 1964, with God's help, I have been waging a continuing battle with cancer. There have been seven operations along the way, radiation, a good many visits to the hospital, and chemotherapy. There have been low moments, of course, as when an ileostomy became necessary, but there also have been encouraging and exciting times. Like so many others, I am deeply grateful for the advances of medical science in our time and also for the prayers of earnest Christians.

It is appropriate to write about illness, because it may be

of benefit not only to those who are ill now but also to other readers. Sooner or later all of us will experience illness of one kind or another, for no one is exempt from illness.

A Look at History

Some historians say that the Black Death which swept Europe in the fourteenth century killed as much as a third of the population. It is beyond our imagination to consider the enormous effect of the pestilence on a whole civilization that waited hopelessly as the plague marched on. Those who survived must have spent their days waiting and burying their dead. This plague, which came again and again and in successive waves, was only one of the many epidemics which has swept across the world with no regard to boundaries or color or religion.

The good news of the twentieth century has been the retreat of many of the dreaded diseases. Polio, typhoid, diptheria, and smallpox have all but disappeared. Our increased knowledge of sanitation, hygiene, and medical technology has placed them all in retreat. In the past two decades the mortality rate of children has been cut in half. Deaths from heart disease for all ages have dropped 22 percent since 1968. Last year, in the United States, tuberculosis, diptheria, poliomyelitis, and gastroenteritis produced a combined death toll of 10,000 lives. If the death rate for those diseases were the same today as in 1900, those diseases would have claimed 800,000 lives.

This, of course, is news worth celebrating. We can scarcely imagine what new discoveries are yet to come, for, between 1965 and 1979, we have increased our expenditures on health care from 39 billion dollars to 139 billion dollars. We think of medical advancement as we think of the relentless march of an army. What will be next among the world's diseases to surrender to this advance? Will it be heart disease, cancer, or the common cold? We have advanced with such amazing success that we easily get the impression that soon every illness will be stamped out.

This is an illusion which accompanies our appreciation of advances in medical science. Because we live in an age when pills are supposed to take away every pain and when penicillin can be counted on to fight infection, the illusion is that illness is in retreat. We tend to feel that illness is becoming so rare that it will never affect us, or our children, or our wives or husbands. Medical science has made its progress, but in the end we will have our share of suffering and illness. Someone has said, "It's a sad day when you wake up and discover that you have a body."

An Example of Courage

Norman Cousins, the influential writer and editor of *Saturday Review*, has recently told an amazing story of his fight with debilitating illness in *Anatomy of an Illness*. The book was written in 1979, but it tells the story of a struggle that took place in 1964. In August of that year Cousins returned from a trip abroad with fever and a general feeling of achiness. Within a week he had difficulty moving his neck, arms, hands, fingers, and legs. He went to the doctor for tests, and the result was disturbing indeed. The infection in his blood system was so great that the doctors could predict nothing better than one chance in 500 of his survival.

What goes on in one's mind when he hears such threatening news? At first, Cousins remembered his experiences as the illness developed. He recalled the abnormal stress and exhaustion that had preceded the illness as he was on his tour abroad. He could not dismiss from his mind that the illness had been activated by his own stress and exhaustion.

Then he began thinking of the future. Would he accept the doctor's assessment of his chances? The answer was a definite no. And he was fortunate enough to have a physician who would appreciate and support his total determination to live. He read everything there was to read about his condition. Then he made a fateful decision. Having read that practically all painkilling drugs have dangerous side effects, he decided to stop taking the mountains of drugs which were prescribed for him each day—even if it involved experiencing more pain.

What was most impressive about Cousins's way of coping was that he simply did not accept the doctor's verdict. He was possessed, as his doctor later conceded, by an extraordinary will to live. This will to live meant that he was not to be "trapped in a cycle of fear, depression, and panic that frequently accompanies the supposedly incurable disease."

Many medical researchers have acknowledged that the will to live may be the most important ingredient in surviving a potentially fatal illness—certainly as important in many situations as the most recent wonder drugs. It is the will to live that mobilizes all of the resources of the body and mind to combat the disease. There are many instances in which apparently hopeless cases, under rather primitive conditions, have survived primarily because they would not accept defeat.

Norman Cousins determined from the very beginning that it was up to him to set in motion the process of allowing the body's own resources to restore his health. He saw himself as the doctor's partner in setting this process in motion. Some of his methods were highly unorthodox: because some researchers had suggested the therapeutic value of laughter in enhancing the right body chemistry, he tried the regular use of therapy through laughter. The belly laughs actually had a positive effect on pain! He was convinced that laughter, as difficult as it might be in these circumstances, had a therapeutic effect. The result is that Cousins is still writing his regular column in *Saturday Review* and telling this story.

Helpful Observations

I am not writing as an expert in medicine or medical technology. Nor do I claim to know if Mr. Cousins's system is the real answer to illness, for I am convinced that there is much yet to be learned about illness. But I am deeply impressed with some of the observations made by this man who refused to capitulate when he was told that it was time to surrender.

I am impressed, in the first place, by his observation that we bear some responsibility for our own healing. Coping with illness involves our own responsibility in many cases. In altogether too many instances, our illnesses are a result of our style of life: our exposure to pollutants, smoking and the consumption of alcohol, poor eating habits and faulty nutrition, and the stress of a hectic life that is controlled by the demands of the clock. A wiser lifestyle—giving up smoking, watching our diet, and being more active physically—would obviously improve our health.

I do not think any reasonable person would suggest that we are always responsible for our own health, for the truth is that there are disorders that we cannot understand and cannot trace back to our lifestyle. There is still much about illness and health that we simply do not understand.

Another of Mr. Cousins's observations is becoming clearer all the time. In research about illness, it is becoming more and more evident that many of our illnesses are so closely tied to our mental and spiritual condition that we can no longer assume that the answer to an illness is the simple prescription for surgery that takes away our symptoms. The state of the mind is also related in an important way. There is a close correlation between the basic attitudes toward life and our ability to overcome illness. Our bodies must be affected by the condition of our souls. We have learned increasingly that a healthy spiritual condition is a precondition for healing.

Holistic Medicine

One of the great movements in medicine in recent years is called the holistic movement. Its purpose is to remind us that health concerns the whole person. It concerns our nutrition, our attitudes, and our sense of well-being. Our spiritual wholeness affects our response to disease and our capacity to cope. I believe that the holistic movement has learned something very important. In fact, as a Christian minister, I am pleased that the whole person and his spiritual needs are receiving serious attention. Perhaps proponents of holistic medicine have succeeded in opening the door to a truth which Christians had discovered in the Scriptures.

I do not believe that holistic medicine has discovered the whole truth of coping with illness. For that truth we must turn to the pages of the Scriptures, for there we meet real people who had to ask the question, "How do I cope with illness?" And they found some answers in their faith.

The Bible and Illness

There is a real sense in which the Bible is a book about, or even by, sick people. In the Bible we meet people who suffered from blindness, lameness, and even epilepsy. The one major figure who wrote a major part of the New Testament suffered from a debilitating chronic illness which he calls his "thorn in the flesh." These sick people had one thing in common: the outcry for relief from their illnesses. Some found their relief in the healing touch of Jesus. Others learned to cope with their illnesses. But whether they found total healing or had to cope with their illnesses, the New Testament tells us that they found a power through faith which undergirded their lives.

Someone has observed that a typical scene in the ministry of Jesus resembled a hospital ward more than anything else.

The Gospel writers indicated that wherever Jesus went, people brought their sick and diseased friends to him. The cry of blind Bartimaeus: "Jesus, Son of David, have mercy on me!" was a typical outcry (Mark 10:47). "If you can do anything, have pity on us and help us" (Mark 9:22) was the cry of an anguished father. These stories tell us in clear terms that the gospel was for sick people. Jesus was the one who said, "Your faith has made you well." Jesus was the Great Physician.

No one can read these stories and think of Jesus as one whose only concern was with organic disturbances. What we notice about him most was his concern with the total person. He reached out and touched people as a gesture of concern. He not only healed blind eyes and deaf ears, but also put lives back together. To a lame man he once said, "Your sins are forgiven" (Mark 2:5), for he wished to put the man's total life back together.

I am happy to see the developments which have been taking place in holistic medicine, but I am convinced that we are never really holistic until we take into account a man's relationship with God. When you read the stories of Jesus, you recognize that God cares for both our mental and our spiritual health. He listens to our cries, and he answers our prayers for help and strength.

But things do not always work out the way we desire. We certainly wish that every outcry in a time of illness resulted in release from pain. But it does not always happen. In the New Testament, not every cry for help resulted in relief. We are fortunate to have the apostle Paul's account of his struggle with chronic illness. We do not know what that illness was, but we do know that it was severe. "Three times I besought the Lord about this, that it should leave me," writes Paul (II Cor. 12:8). Three prayers were a sign of special urgency. But the thorn in the flesh did not go away. Paul was left to cope with his illness.

How Do We Determine the Good?

Here I should like to observe that, contrary to our first thoughts about the matter, illnesses can serve good purposes. Whatever brings us closer to God is good. Whatever causes us to develop the inner, spiritual qualities of life is good. Though illness itself may not be good, the results often are good. Lives are made stronger. Our spirituality becomes deeper. Illness can pull us away from the trivialities of life and center our thoughts on the primary issues of living. If considered in the right way, an illness may be a great blessing.

It all depends on how we cope with illness. The remarkable fact in the story of Paul's life is the way in which he coped with his illness. Coping did not involve giving up in self-pity. Paul related the story of his thorn in the flesh in order to tell us that his weakness—his physical ailment—had been the occasion for the working of the power of God. Paul had prayed that the ailment might be taken away. But the only answer he got was, "My grace is sufficient for you, for my power is made perfect in weakness" (II Cor. 12:9). Paul had found his sickness to be not a handicap but an opportunity for the power of God. That was Paul's way of coping.

Then we go on to recall the rugged itinerary of the man who was "handicapped" with a dreadful illness. Coping involved keeping a schedule of travels which would have been exhausting for any healthy person. As he later wrote, "Five times I have received at the hands of the Jews the forty lashes less one. Three times I have been beaten with rods; once I was stoned. Three times I have been shipwrecked; a night and a day I have been adrift at sea; on frequent journeys, in danger from rivers, danger from robbers, danger from my own people, danger from Gentiles, danger in the city, danger in the wilderness, danger at sea, danger from false brethren; in toil and hardship, through many a sleepless night, in hunger and thirst, often without food, in cold and exposure" (II Cor. 11:24–27). Illness did not turn him inward in self-pity. He could find, even in illness, the God-given strength to triumph over all these hindrances.

Goals to Achieve

One of the vital ingredients in working through an illness is to be found in being caught up in a mission that is larger than ourselves. It is this quality which I see in Paul on a grand scale. This missionary, caught up in the plan of God, would not allow a chronic illness to stop him. To be sure, his illness was a nagging nuisance. Undoubtedly he was able to go on during many difficult days only by the inner strength which came through his trust in God.

When illness comes, there is often opportunity to think more seriously than usual about one's life. In such contemplation it is quite likely that a person may find himself in need not only of physical healing but also of spiritual healing. The important first step in overcoming illness, whether it be physical or spiritual, is to make sure that one is in a right relationship with God. This begins when one believes in Jesus Christ as the divine Son of God and accepts him as Lord and Savior. This belief needs to be a decision of will to turn away from the sins of the world and to direct one's life toward the good, wholesome, and righteous things of life. At that point, baptism signifies the death of the old sinful person and the birth of the new person. All past sins are forgiven and one begins a new life with his Lord. There follows confidence, assurance, and encouragement to face physical illness or any of life's other emergencies. More important than the healing of the body is Christ's unique ability to heal the soul.

The Bible is not a book which offers instant solutions to our problems of disease and health. Paul was not healed.

Timothy was not miraculously delivered from stomach trouble, nor was Epaphroditus. But they found in their faith the experience of being caught up in the plan of God. Those who were not healed still found meaning in their lives in the fact that they were a part of a great plan which was greater than they.

All of us have sometime heard the lines of the famous prayer: "God, grant me the courage to change the things which should be changed, the serenity to accept the things which cannot be changed, and the wisdom to know the difference." This prayer is a way of coping with illness. Trusting God, we do all within our power to overcome illness. If that fails, we continue to trust God to help us with whatever comes. With the apostle Paul we conclude, "I have learned, in whatever state I am, to be content. . . . I can do all things in him who strengthens me" (Phil. 4:11, 13).

13

When the Worst Happens

Harold Hazelip

"The earth stood still the day my doctor told me I had cancer. I remember the walls in my hospital room were a sickly pink. It was an emotional shock to me and my family unlike any other we had experienced. I couldn't think straight." This report of a cancer patient tells about the numbness, the confusion, and the loneliness when we fear the worst is going to happen.

Such experiences are rare for most of us. But we have a nagging fear of tragedy. The ringing of a telephone in the wee hours of the night, the perplexed look on a doctor's face as he studies our chart, a son or daughter being late unnerves us. A voice deep inside us asks, "What if your daughter fails to return from her date, or the cyst is malignant, or the investment you made last year is worthless?" Which is more troubling—experiencing tragedy or fearing that we will?

What if the "worst" happens? The event itself—personal illness, loss of a loved one, international upheaval—is often beyond our control. But how shall we respond? The writer of the New Testament book called Hebrews describes those "who all their lives were held in slavery by their fear of death" (Heb. 2:15, NIV).

Is there some way to lift this smothering fear of death that creeps in to spoil our lives?

Our Response to Tragedy

A recent article in *National Geographic* traced the impact of the Mount St. Helen's volcano. Here was a photograph of a young woman, eyes set with worry, face stained with tears. Her father was missing. Happily, he came back safely. At that moment, it did not matter that the woman's father was safe. Her world had been invaded by the chilling possibility that her father was dead, perhaps buried under volcanic ash.

Each of us responds differently to crisis. That response may say a great deal about our inner selves. Tragedy tends to tear open the soul, revealing good and evil, strength and weakness.

When bad news comes, the usual immediate response is a penetrating numbness. Our senses are anesthetized. Our minds try to understand what our ears have heard. One person explained, "It's like being a spectator to your actions." This numbing of the senses allows us to function and to do the necessary in the face of intense personal pain.

The next step is often a denial of what has happened. "It can't be," we say. "I feel fine; you must have the wrong x-rays." Or we say, "I saw him only yesterday." One physician reports that her patients have partial deafness when she tries to describe their illnesses. After years of working with seriously ill patients, she assumes that a patient will hear only one-third of what she says about his condition. Denial may help us absorb bad news slowly, but it can cause problems. It may make us delay treatment until the disease is no longer curable.

As we search for a reason for this catastrophe, we may become angry with life. A terrible disease reaches out and says to us, "Tag! You're it!" We may blame God, family members, or the hospital staff. The Old Testament prophet Jeremiah cried out to God, "Why is my pain unending and my wound grievous and incurable? Will you be to me like a deceptive brook, like a spring that fails?" (Jer. 15:18, NIV).

Anger may have a good effect on us if it causes us to take our stand no matter what comes. Once a family was shipwrecked in the mid-Pacific with a little water and not much else. They sighted a cargo ship and began to set off signal flares as the vessel approached. Amazingly, the crew of the ship failed to respond and sailed into the horizon. The father remembered his feelings: "I surveyed the empty flare cartons bitterly . . . and something happened to me in that instant that for me changed the whole aspect of our predicament. If these seamen couldn't rescue us, then we would have to make it on our own. . . . I felt a strength flooding through me, lifting me from the depression to a state of almost cheerful abandon." Anger can be petty, or it may have a heroic quality that helps us rise above self-pity and depression.

Perhaps our worst response to tragedy is self-pity. The latest pain is merely additional evidence that life is not worthwhile. We are tempted to give up, to quit trying. Self-pity may take the form of guilt; we imagine that this sickness or loss is a punishment for our sins. Jesus would not allow all suffering to be explained as immediate punishment for sin. "[He] sends rain on the just and the unjust," he observed (Matt. 5:45). He pointed to a tragedy in his day: "Those eighteen who died when the tower in Siloam fell on them—do you think they were more guilty than all the others living in Jerusalem? I tell you, no! But unless you repent, you too will all perish" (Luke 13:4–5, NIV). The fact that you suffer does not mean that you are guilty of some terrible wrong.

Seriously ill people often begin to feel worthless. Dr. Lawrence LeShan has given years of emotional support to cancer victims and their families. He asked one patient,

"What do you think it is that makes you so angry at yourself—that makes you feel so guilty? Do you feel that you have done something to deserve this?" She replied, "No, I've done nothing. You don't understand, Doctor. It's not that I've been or done anything. It's that I've done nothing and been nothing." Such hopelessness cannot be driven back with medical expertise. Something must reach deeply into the self and allow one to declare again that life is worth battling to save. When the worst happens, a person must ask, "What is my life? And how shall I live it in good times and bad?"

Our Quest for Understanding

When tragedy comes, we seize reason by the throat and demand answers to our questions: "Why me? Why now?"

The quest for understanding has its pitfalls. We may presume that answers must be instant, like parcels from a vending machine. When answers do not come easily, it is tempting to try the other door—despair and hopelessness.

On the other hand, without the desire to understand, we would know much less about how to control disease or disaster. To a large degree, our Western scientific enterprise is founded on the biblical notion of a world of order and predictability, even if at times we do not understand it.

For instance, Laura Lue Claypool was a bright, happy child who at the age of eight was extremely active. One morning she seemed especially tired, but her parents assumed that she had overexerted herself. When she experienced swelling in her ankle, they sought medical care. The diagnosis: acute leukemia. Eighteen months and ten days later she died.

Laura Lue's father is a minister. At first he grappled with the "why" of leukemia and death itself. He later wrote that he had not found any single answer that settles all the questions or accounts for all the nuances of this tragedy.

As he struggled with his loss, he came to appreciate the pain of Abraham who was called to offer Isaac, his son, as a sacrifice. Isaac was a child of promise, born to aged parents. Abraham had done nothing to merit having this son. God gave him as a free gift. Life is a gift, not a deserved possession.

Claypool understood this better when he recalled an old green Bendix washing machine loaned to his family during World War II. After it had been in the basement for a few years, he forgot its true owner and was shocked when the owner came back for it. His mother reminded him that the machine had never belonged to their family. Their use of it had been a gift. Instead of being angry that it was taken away, she said, the family should be grateful that they had had it at all.

The New Testament's Response

Our claims on life are fragile. Life is God's gift, not our right. Much of the battle as we face tragedy is with ourselves—our fear, our hopelessness. But the New Testament is a book of hope, of victory over our worst fears.

Harry Emerson Fosdick once observed, "The New Testament is full of trouble. It begins with a massacre of innocent children. . . . It ends with a vision in which the souls of martyred saints under the altar cry, 'How long, O Master?' " Living in a time when life was cheap and misfortune was plentiful, the writers of the New Testament made three significant responses to trouble.

First, God knows and cares about man's misfortune. Not even a sparrow can fall to the earth without his knowledge.

Not only does God care, but he also chose to involve himself in humanity's pains. His only Son was described as "a man of sorrows and acquainted with grief" (Isa. 53:3). As C. S. Dinsmore expresses it, "There was a cross in the heart of God before there was one planted on the green hill outside of Jerusalem."

Jesus neither gave long explanations of evil nor ignored it. His ministry was an all-out assault on the kingdom of darkness. He declared, "The Spirit of the Lord is upon me, because he has anointed me to preach good news to the poor. He has sent me to proclaim release to the captives and recovering of sight to the blind, to set at liberty those who are oppressed, to proclaim the acceptable year of the Lord" (Luke 4:18–19).

Jesus did not simply make speeches. He made no cheap promises. He faced his own struggle in Gethsemane with the unseen opponent: fear of death. Armed only with the Word of his God, he faced an angry mob, a cynical governor, and the taunts of petty public officials. He died with words of trust on his lips: "Father, into thy hands I commit my spirit!" (Luke 23:46).

Jesus dared to look death in the eye. When we talk about the worst that can happen to us, our fear of death and oblivion is close at hand. Ray Bradbury captured the power of this fear in *Something Wicked This Way Comes*. In the novel, Cooger and Dark's Pandemonium Shadow Show comes to a small Midwestern town. It is greeted with the enthusiasm reserved for circuses and carnivals. But this is no ordinary carnival. A merry-go-round that reverses the aging process, a mirror that captures souls, and a wax museum of living people convince two boys that this show is evil to the core. Townspeople are offered eternal youth. They accept, only to discover that their new condition is worse than the original one. One of the characters says, "There is nothing we are so slapstick with as our immortal souls." Faced with death, people are likely to make some bad bargains. For a time it seems that the evil forces will prevail. Only one thing saves the townspeople—laughter. Instead of accepting this bargain, Charles Halloway begins to laugh at the shadowy

Mr. Dark. Then the entire evil armada is thrown into disarray.

That is fiction. But Paul describes the real work of Jesus: "He disarmed the principalities and powers and made a public example of them, triumphing over them [in the cross]" (Col. 2:15).

The final affirmation of the New Testament is that the question of victory is not *if* but *when*. Jesus' resurrection has destroyed the power of death. The Book of Hebrews says, "Since the children have flesh and blood, he too shared in their humanity so that by his death he might destroy him who holds the power of death—that is, the devil—and free those who all their lives were held in slavery by their fear of death" (Heb. 2:14–15, NIV). We face an unknown future with confidence, knowing that ". . . he who is in [us] is greater than he who is in the world" (I John 4:4). Armed with this knowledge, Christians have stood through the centuries in the face of misfortune and disaster. Pain is real, but it is not absolute.

George Frederick Handel's biographer tells of a crucial time in Handel's life: "His health and his fortunes had reached the lowest ebb. His right side had become paralyzed, and his money was all gone. His creditors seized him and threatened him with imprisonment. For a brief time he was tempted to give up the fight—but then he rebounded again to compose the greatest of his inspirations, the epic Messiah." The "Hallelujah Chorus" was written by a broken, poverty-stricken man.

When the worst happens, we are seldom prepared for it. Our inexperience in facing difficulty troubles us. But to acknowledge that all of life is a gift will free us from making demands about how life must be. Realizing that God knows and cares, that Jesus has experienced our sorrows, and that he has guaranteed our victory in him gives us the strength to carry on when the worst happens.

We are free to join the caravan of those who can say with

the apostle Paul, "But we have this treasure in jars of clay to show that this all-surpassing power is from God and not from us. We are hard pressed on every side, but not crushed; perplexed, but not in despair; persecuted, but not abandoned; struck down, but not destroyed. We always carry around in our body the death of Jesus, so that the life of Jesus may also be revealed in our body" (II Cor. 4:7–10, NIV).

14

"Why Go On?"

Joe R. Barnett

In February 1975, one of America's most admired religious leaders died in old age after a distinguished career. He had been a professor and, later, president of one of the nation's most prestigious seminaries. His influence had been felt throughout the world through the hundreds of students who had studied under him. He had written many articles and books, and had been a moral spokesman for numerous causes. But there was something shocking about his death.

On January 29, Elizabeth Van Dusen, his wife, died from an overdose of sleeping pills. Henry Van Dusen, the distinguished religious leader, escaped the same death only because he failed to digest the pills. He lingered on until February 13, when heart failure did what the pills had failed to do.

Shock waves of concern were felt wherever this distinguished man was known. How could anyone take his own life, especially a renowned moral spokesman? The deceased couple left a simple note to explain their action: "We are both increasingly weak and unwell, and who would want to die in a nursing home?"

In the face of advancing age and increasing infirmities, they asked, "Why go on?" Self-inflicted death was their answer to the question. Life was no longer worth the struggle.

Is it right to commit suicide when life becomes a burden—filled with seemingly unsolvable problems, or frustrating loneliness, or a sense of worthlessness?

The Ultimate "How-to" Book

Most any bookstore today has an entire section of "how-to" books: *How to Repair Your Own Car, How to Lose Weight, How to Increase Your Vocabulary*. Now, according to a *Newsweek* article (April 1980), the ultimate self-help book is on the market. Entitled *A Guide to Self-Deliverance*, it is a book about how to commit suicide.

This controversial book was published in England by Exit, a six-thousand-member organization dedicated to the right to "die with dignity." The editors said the book is a response to popular demand. They argue that since it is illegal for doctors to practice "mercy killing" (euthanasia) the only alternative for the terminally ill is to "do it yourself." Thousands have requested the manual.

The Frightening Increase of Suicide

Even in the Bible we observe instances of self-inflicted death. Saul, the first king of Israel, fell on his own sword rather than be taken in battle (I Sam. 31:4). And there was Judas, who betrayed Jesus.

So suicide isn't new. The fact that it is being treated as a legitimate option is disturbing. The increased number of suicides in our society is especially distressing. Suicide is the number-two cause of death among college and university students, second only to traffic fatalities. At some of our largest universities the tallest buildings on campus are tightly secured.

And suicide is increasing among teenagers. Suicide is the

third leading cause of death among children and teenagers, just behind accidents and murder. In the past decade the suicide rate has risen by 100 percent. According to some estimates, fifty-seven American children and teenagers attempt suicide every hour. The rate of attempted suicides reported is three times the number twenty years ago.

Suicide, Companion of Affluence

It is revealing to observe the circumstances under which suicide becomes prevalent. Studies show that the number of suicides decreases in wartime—in the presence of actual danger to life. And suicide is not a major problem among the very poor who daily struggle for survival. Eugene Genovese, in his history of slavery, *Roll, Jordan, Roll: The World the Slaves Made*, points out that slaves never commited suicide in large numbers, even under the most miserable conditions.

The fact is that the suicide rate rises as affluence increases. The wealthiest countries in the world have the highest rates of suicide. According to the latest issue of the *Encyclopedia Britannica*, suicide is the companion of a high standard of living, advanced age, and loneliness. It is also the companion of secularization and urbanization. Where there is deep religious faith and a simple lifestyle, the suicide rate tends to decrease. It is sobering to observe that self-destruction goes with those things we often call "civilization"—life in the city and a high standard of living.

Why? Viktor Frankl, in *The Unheard Cry for Meaning*, suggests one answer. He tells of an American university where sixty students were asked why they had attempted suicide. Eighty-five percent said it was because life was meaningless. Frankl writes, "For too long we have been dreaming a dream from which we are now waking up: the dream that if we just improve the socioeconomic situation of people everything will be okay and people will be happy.

The truth is, as the struggle for survival has subsided, the question has emerged: survival for what?"

On the other hand, most of us have seen inspiring examples of people who were happy under adverse circumstances. I know people who look back to the depression or the war years, despite all the deprivation of those times, with a sense of nostalgia. There were goals to be pursued—and those goals made it worth going on.

Who Cares?

I want to suggest one more reason why suicide is viewed as a legitimate option today. This reason is poignantly described in Thomas Hardy's *Jude the Obscure*. There is a scene in which Jude and Susan had just discovered the lifeless bodies of their three children hanging in the chamber room of the inn where they were staying. The oldest boy, young Jude, had left a note saying, "Doing it because we are too menny." Susan blamed herself because she had talked with young Jude of the burden which came with a new child on the way.

Can it be that self-destruction is the response of those who believe they are superfluous?

Studies of child suicide have shown that child abuse was not the cause; the cause was ambivalence. No one seemed to care whether these children lived or died. Many people are convinced that their continued existence will be a burden. Why go on when our lives are a burden to others?

Who Is in Control?

In Dostoevsky's novel *The Possessed*, one of the characters, a young revolutionary, argues that suicide may actually be a heroic act, for he says it is the supreme act of freedom. It is the way of governing my own life, he says—of being my own master. He says it is not true that life must go on, for my own self-destruction is my way of being supremely free. There is a sense in which he was right, for suicide is the path of those who refuse to place themselves in anyone's hands—even God's.

As I read the Bible, it becomes clear to me that the Christian is not to be particularly afraid of death. There is that poignant scene of Jesus in the Garden of Gethsemane as he felt the agony of facing the suffering he was about to experience. He chose to go to Jerusalem to face his own death. Even so, he prayed to God, "If it be possible, let this cup pass from me" (Matt. 26:39).

The thought of the approaching suffering was painful to him. He was *willing* to die, but he didn't *want* to die.

The story continued in the lives of the apostles, and those in the early church. Observers were shocked that Christians willingly and courageously met death. Christians never invited death—but if it had to come, they accepted it. However, they never tried to take it into their own hands.

This is quite different from people who decide life just isn't worth it. There is one thing which the suicides of the Bible had in common: they refused to let God rule their lives. Saul wanted to be king in his own way, not in God's way. Judas could not accept the kind of discipleship Jesus demanded, so he chose to go his own way. Both refused to place themselves in God's hands.

Should Life Go On?

There are important reasons why life should go on. For one thing, life is a gift from the Creator. We did not perpetrate our birth, and we have no right to perpetrate our death.

But there is an even more compelling reason why life should go on. It centers in the fact that in Jesus Christ we have been loved. We cannot despair of life, however much it may seem unsuccessful, unhappy, or useless. To throw life away is to reject the love which has been lavished on us. There is no great tragedy in dying, but there is great tragedy in dying for the wrong reason.

A Caring Community

Those who ask "why go on?" often raise the question because they are convinced they are a burden. Perhaps we have contributed to that feeling of despair. If our only concern is our pleasure and a higher standard of living we easily become annoyed by those who are too young or too old to make it on their own. How utterly tragic is a society that can tolerate no burdens. We enter life as a burden, and we may depart it that way. If there were no burdens in our society—none of the very young, the very old, or the very distressed—we would hardly be a human community at all.

Earlier I mentioned the book about slavery, *Roll, Jordan, Roll*. The author points out that those who live under the most oppressive circumstances often have the most defiant will to live. One of the reasons is that they are in a community of love and concern. They wish to survive because they belong to a community which cares.

Perhaps this kind of community is what is missing in the lives of those who ask, "Why go on?" In the midst of a great metropolis this kind of caring community may be difficult to find, but it isn't impossible. There are congregations of Christians throughout the world who form a community which "bears one another's burdens." In fact, the church would not be the church if it didn't bring together the old and the young, the married and the single into a caring fellowship. Having this close relationship is a reminder that our life is important to others.

Courage to Continue

The young atheist in Dostoevsky's *Possessed* spoke of the courage of taking your life into your own hands. He was wrong. It takes more courage to live with suffering, to struggle through disappointments, to trust in a future which seems grim.

This courage is available to those who have placed their lives in God's hands. Jesus said, "I came that they might have life, and have it abundantly" (John 10:10). Paul wrote, "When anyone is united to Christ, there is a new world" (II Cor. 5:17, NEB).

Here then is one of the principal values of committing your life to Jesus. Place your faith in him—where it is never misplaced. Repent of those sins which have made life miserable. Be baptized into him. This will give you a new and meaningful life. As the Bible says, "We were buried therefore with him by baptism into death, so that as Christ was raised from the dead by the glory of the Father, we too might walk in *newness* of life" (Rom. 6:4, italics mine). For the Christian, there is a new way of looking at the world.

Those who have studied suicide tell us that the two major reasons people decide they cannot go on any longer are the sense of meaninglessness in their lives and the loneliness which comes from feeling no one cares. In Jesus we have a goal to pursue, a God whose love is real, and a loving community which cares for us. Jesus gives us the courage to live—even in the presence of difficulty and disappointment.

15
Facing Death

Batsell Barrett Baxter

What is the most important question of our time? It seems strange, but Dr. Robert Jay Lifton, Yale University's eminent psychiatrist, says, "Death is the most important question of our time." Ernest Becker, in *Denial of Death*, agrees. Becker advances the thesis that the single greatest task of each human being is facing the inevitability of his own death. Why are we so afraid of death? Why do we avoid talking about death?

Thoughtful observers tell us that we Americans repress all talk and all thought of death. They tell us that just as the people of the Victorian era repressed any discussion of sex, so we moderns repress death and its symbolism. Death is not to be talked of in front of the children, nor talked about at all if we can help it. "Mankind is frightened by the mere word 'death,' and nowhere more so than in America," says English essayist J. B. Priestley. He continues, "At dinner parties there I have brought up the question of death just to study the stunned reactions. Most people switched off the subject as if they were changing channels."

By the use of special terms such as "mortuaries," "slumber rooms," "passed away," "sleeping," "the deceased," "interment," and the like, people generally seem to be trying to avoid recognizing the reality of death. By beautiful caskets, lovely flowers, and the cosmetic restoration of a natural appearance, modern man seems to be trying to camouflage the reality of death. In other times death often took place at home, but today death usually comes in hospitals and goes unobserved except by the very closest of kin. The funeral services are now usually held in funeral chapels, thereby keeping the familiar sites of life untouched by death. All of this seems artificial.

Modern man seems to seek escape from any consideration of death, either by triviality of daily routine or by throwing himself totally into the pursuit of some great cause or achievement. In America we prize youthfulness, vitality, health, and productivity; the trend is to push thoughts about death out of the mind. There are indications, however, that we have not been able to overcome our anxiety. Rather, we may have merely repressed it.

Reactions to Death

For a time consideration of death may be avoided. Yet before long it must be faced. We, or someone we love, will be called to face the reality of death. What do we do then?

Elisabeth Kubler-Ross has pioneered a new field which has taught us much about the experience of dying. Her book, *On Death and Dying*, describes how she learned from dying patients and sought to bring care and comfort to the dying. When she began her work, she found a resistance on the part of the administration and staff, as well as the doctors, in the large Chicago hospital where she began her research. Seemingly no one wanted to talk about death, nor to admit that many of the patients were terminally ill. Gradually Dr. Kubler-Ross was able to lift the silence surrounding death, and when she did, she found patients longing to have someone face the facts honestly with them.

After extensive research Dr. Kubler-Ross tells us that the

terminally ill patient ordinarily goes through five stages. First, the patient refuses to believe the diagnosis: "It must be someone else. You must have read the wrong x-rays." The next stage is anger and bitterness: "Why would God allow this to happen to me?" In the third stage the patient bargains for time: "Oh, God, if you will only give me a few more months, I will be a different person." In the fourth stage the patient is overcome with depression. Finally, the patient accepts his fate. This analysis of the mental pain of accepting one's own death illustrates what the Bible calls "the sting of death" (I Cor. 15:56).

The sting of death has led our generation to use every technological means to try to outwit it. Remarkable progress has been made, for instance, in transplanting vital bodily organs. Lives that only a decade ago would be over are now being extended with heart, kidney, or liver transplants. Now medical researchers are studying the possibility of extending life through the transplants of even the lungs and the brain. Can life be prolonged indefinitely by the use of a supply of spare parts? In addition, medical technology is making progress toward inventing bionic devices which can replace the kidneys, liver, pancreas, and heart.

Since 1965, when Robert Ettinger published *The Prospect of Immortality*, the public has become aware of the idea of cryonic suspension—the quick freezing of one who has just died, with the hope that he can be revived in the future when the illness that killed him becomes curable. The concept seems fanciful, but more than fifty people have attempted to outwit death in this way.

This research may sound as if it belongs to the world of science fiction, and I would not dare to predict what success may come to such efforts to extend the lives of human beings. But the significant fact is that medical science recognizes the truth which is stated in Scripture: Death is the enemy. "All that a man has he will give for his life," says Satan in the Book of Job (2:4). We all know that life is precious.

The Biblical Perspective

The Bible never glosses over or tries to cover up the fact of death. It was Solomon who wrote in the Old Testament Book of Ecclesiastes (3:1–2), "For everything there is a season, and a time for every matter under heaven: a time to be born, and a time to die." The Bible does not minimize the importance of death as the ancient Stoics did or as some of the world religions of our day still do. Christianity takes death seriously. Although we enjoy living, cherish loved ones and friends, work diligently for noble causes, and make the most of the beautiful world about us, we do not hide our eyes from and close our ears to the fact of death. We do not need to, for we recognize death as a part of God's plan for our ultimate good. We accept the only statistic that never varies: one out of one will die. Yet we do not cringe in fear, because we understand the place of death in God's ultimate plan for our lives.

Some fifteen hundred years before the time of Christ, Moses wrote, "The years of our life are threescore and ten, or even by reason of strength fourscore; yet their span is but toil and trouble; they are soon gone, and we fly away. . . . So teach us to number our days that we may get a heart of wisdom" (Ps. 90:10, 12). At a much later time the New Testament writer James asked the question, "What is your life?" Then he gave this simple but accurate answer, "For you are a mist that appears for a little time and then vanishes" (James 4:14). The brevity of life and the inevitability of death are mentioned over and over in the Scriptures, as well they should be.

In speaking of the approach of his own death, Jesus said to his disciples, "The hour has come for the Son of man to be glorified. Truly, truly, I say to you, unless a grain of wheat falls into the earth and dies, it remains alone; but if it dies, it bears much fruit. He who loves his life loses it, and he who hates his life in this world will keep it for eternal life" (John 12:23–25). Jesus also said, "Behold, we are going up to Jerusalem; and the Son of man will be delivered to the chief priests and scribes, and they will condemn him to death, and deliver him to the Gentiles to be mocked and scourged and crucified, and he will be raised on the third day" (Matt. 20:18–19).

To his inner circle of disciples, Jesus also spoke of his imminent death: "Little children, yet a little while I am with you. . . . Let not your hearts be troubled; believe in God, believe also in me. In my Father's house are many rooms; if it were not so, would I have told you that I go to prepare a place for you? And when I go and prepare a place for you, I will come again and will take you to myself, that where I am you may be also" (John 13:33; 14:1–3).

A little earlier, in seeking to assuage the grief of Mary and Martha at the death of their brother, Lazarus, Jesus said, "I am the resurrection and the life; he who believes in me, though he die, yet shall he live. . ." (John 11:25).

Our Resurrection

The Scriptures are explicit in speaking of the resurrection of all men. In writing to the Corinthian Christians, the apostle Paul said, "If for this life only we have hoped in Christ, we are of all men most to be pitied. But in fact Christ has been raised from the dead, the first fruits of those who have fallen asleep. For as by a man came death, by a man has come also the resurrection of the dead. For as in Adam all die, so also in Christ shall all be made alive. But each in his own order: Christ the first fruits, then at his coming those who belong to Christ" (I Cor. 15:19–23).

In a second letter to the church at Corinth, Paul wrote further concerning death: "So we do not lose heart. Though our outer nature is wasting away, our inner nature is being renewed every day. For this slight momentary affliction is preparing for us an eternal weight of glory beyond all comparison, because we look not to the things that are seen but to the things that are unseen; for the things that are seen are transient, but the things that are unseen are eternal. For we know that if the earthly tent we live in is destroyed, we have a building from God, a house not made with hands, eternal in the heavens" (II Cor. 4:16–5:1).

Paul more fully explained death and the resurrection in his first letter to the Thessalonians, "But we would not have you ignorant, brethren, concerning those who are asleep, that you may not grieve as others do who have no hope. For since we believe that Jesus died and rose again, even so, through Jesus, God will bring with him those who have fallen asleep. For this we declare to you by the word of the Lord, that we who are alive, who are left until the coming of the Lord, shall not precede those who have fallen asleep. For the Lord himself will descend from heaven with a cry of command, with the archangel's call, and with the sound of the trumpet of God. And the dead in Christ will rise first; then we who are alive, who are left, shall be caught up together with them in the clouds to meet the Lord in the air; and so we shall always be with the Lord. Therefore comfort one another with these words" (I Thess. 4:13–18).

It was in view of this understanding of death to be followed by an even better life that Paul could say of himself, "For me to live is Christ, and to die is gain. . . . I am hard pressed between the two. My desire is to depart and be with Christ, for that is far better. But to remain in the flesh is more necessary on your account" (Phil. 1:21, 23–24).

The apostle Peter also wrote concerning Christ's resurrection and its significance for us. "Blessed be the God and Father of our Lord Jesus Christ! By his great mercy we have been born anew to a living hope through the resurrection of Jesus Christ from the dead, and to an inheritance which is imperishable, undefiled, and unfading, kept in heaven for you, who by God's power are guarded through faith for a salvation ready to be revealed in the last time. In this you rejoice. . ." (I Peter 1:3–6).

The Old Testament psalmist wrote, "Precious in the sight of the LORD is the death of his saints" (Ps. 116:15). In the final book of the Bible is this parallel statement, " 'Blessed are the dead who die in the Lord henceforth.' 'Blessed indeed,' says the Spirit, 'that they may rest from their labors, for their deeds follow them!' " (Rev. 14:13). In that same book of the Bible there are also these hope-filled words, "He will wipe away every tear from their eyes, and death shall be no more, neither shall there be mourning nor crying nor pain any more, for the former things have passed away" (Rev. 21:4). It is in view of these great promises of a better life beyond death that the Christian faces death in confidence and hope rather than in doubt and despair.

The Christian View of Death

According to the Bible, death is best understood as another experience of birth. When our lives began, we lived in the narrow confines of our mothers' bodies. We developed our capacities of hearing and seeing which could not be used in that place. Then we were born, dying in a small sense of that word, but at the same time thrust into a larger realm of life.

Now we are developing capacities which are not fully exhausted in this brief life—love for God and others. Death will bring us, if we are God's children, into a still larger experience of life. John wrote, "Beloved, we are God's children now; it does not yet appear what we shall be, but we know that when he appears we shall be like him, for we shall see him as he is" (I John 3:2).

We all will die. But death is another experience of birth for the Christian. We emerge in the other world in the care and keeping of God. The really important death for each of us occurs during this physical life when we die to sin and become alive to God. Paul wrote, "How can we who died to sin still live in it? Do you not know that all of us who have been baptized into Christ Jesus were baptized into his death? We were buried therefore with him by baptism into death, so that as Christ was raised from the dead by the glory of the Father, we too might walk in newness of life" (Rom. 6:2–4). With our trust in God, we allow ourselves to be buried in baptism, as Jesus was buried in the tomb. Then we are brought forth into the new, more wonderful Christian life. Later, physical death means only a change in our environment and is relatively unimportant. Paul described Jesus as the one "who abolished death and brought life and immortality to light through the gospel" (II Tim. 1:10).

About A.D. 125, Aristides, a Greek writer, explained to a friend the success of a new religion he had become acquainted with: "If any righteous man among the Christians passes from this world, they rejoice and offer thanks to God and they escort his body with songs and thanksgiving as if he were setting out from one place to another nearby."

As Death Approaches

Perhaps you have had the experience of calming a small child who was afraid of the dark. The child's perceptions of the shadows can change remarkably when a loving parent stands by to give assurance that no harm will come. The faithful promise of the parent gives the child the peace of mind to face the darkness. It is the same way with us. We too face the shadow of fear caused by death. Because we trust the One who has conquered death, we can face the future with the confidence that we will not be harmed. Our real assurance, as death approaches, rests on the character of God, and on the teachings, the promises, and the example of Jesus.

Roland Perdue, in a manuscript meaningfully titled "I

Will Die, But Death Will Never Hold Me," tells this story: "During a night of fire bombing (in the days of the Blitz of London) a father and his small son ran from their burning house. Seeking some form of shelter, the father jumped into a shell hole in the yard and then he held up his arms for his son to follow. But the small boy, hearing the father's voice urging him to jump, replied, 'But I can't see you.' The father could see the child outlined against the night sky and the flickering flames, and he answered, 'But I can see you. Jump.' The faith by which and in which we live and which enables us to conduct our living and dying with dignity is not that we can see, but that we are seen; not that we can know without doubt, but that we are known by the God who is Lord of us in both our living and in our dying. For nothing can separate us from his love."

"Be Ye Also Ready"

The Christian is so in tune with spiritual things and so intimate with the Lord that he neither fears nor dreads death. Each of us should strive to live in a state of readiness in case the end should come suddenly. When Christ was on the earth, he admonished his disciples, ". . . you also must be ready; for the Son of man is coming at an hour you do not expect" (Matt. 24:44). A little later he added, "Watch therefore, for you know neither the day nor the hour" (Matt. 25:13).

This means, of course, that we need to have not only the superficial elements of our lives ready if the end should come suddenly, but also the deeper things. It is fine to have all of our business and personal things in good shape, but it is infinitely more important for our souls to be ready to meet God in judgment.

This means that we must have become children of God, in the manner prescribed in the New Testament, and that we must be living faithful, obedient lives, serving God and our fellow men. The ideal is to believe early in life that Jesus Christ is the divine Son of God and to decide to follow Christ. This means repentance, or turning away from the world and its sin; this means the confession of Christ before men; this means obedience to the Lord's command to be baptized. Then it means living as Christ lived—in purity and in concern for the needs of others. While it is ideal to begin early in life, it is never too late to begin. One is never too old to have a genuine desire to follow Christ and to be willing to obey him.

The only ultimate tragedy of life is to die outside of Christ. What a blessing to know that not one of us need be lost. Christ died that we might live, and invites us to come to him and to share eternal life in heaven. As the Christian faces death, he may well remember the words of the poet John Milton, "[Death is the] golden key/That opes the palace of Eternity."

Epilogue
Quiet Time

Harold Hazelip

The Bible has many things to say about the value of silence. "Be still and know that I am God," says the psalmist (Ps. 46:10). "The LORD is in his holy temple; let all the earth keep silence before him" (Hab. 2:20). "Commune with your own hearts on your beds, and be silent" (Ps. 4:4). "Be silent, all flesh, before the LORD" (Zech. 2:13). In the words of Ecclesiastes, there is "a time to keep silence, and a time to speak" (3:7). We must discover the resources in silence that keep the world from being "too much with us." We must find time to shut out the distractions and the noise and recover our sense of direction.

Jesus said it another way. "When you pray, you must not be like the hypocrites; for they love to stand and pray in the synagogues and at the street corners, that they may be seen by men. . . . But when you pray, go into your room and shut the door and pray to your Father who is in secret" (Matt. 6:5–6). Jesus knew that there was a time for public prayer, for he himself worshiped regularly with others. But he also knew that there was a time to be alone with God, to talk with him in solitude.

A Time for Prayer

I am struck by the assumption which seems to lie behind Jesus' words, "when you pray." It was unthinkable to Jesus that his disciples would not have the time for private prayer. He did not say, "if you should pray," but "when you pray." He assumed that they would pray—perhaps at fixed times in the day. In fact, Jewish tradition expected faithful people to pray three times daily. Surely Jesus expected nothing less.

I am impressed by the regularity and discipline that Jesus expected from his disciples. The idea of regular hours of prayer and meditation may seem foreign to us. Of course, it is true that we may pray at any time. But "anytime" can easily come to mean "at no time," for our schedules become crowded and we may forget. Surely there would be great value in having a regular time to pray, which we would guard as carefully as we do the dates in our appointment books.

But how do you find the time for regular meditation and prayer? We ask the question in all seriousness, for we find ourselves juggling a hundred different commitments. Can we "squeeze in" a quiet time? The very question shows the disproportion of our lives. If we are searching for time to meditate, then countless other things have already taken priority in our lives.

I am impressed by Helmut Thielicke's suggestion that our failure to find a quiet time for reflection suggests that we are more at home with the routine concerns of the day that fill our time. The letter we received, the tax notice that came in the mail, the promotion we wanted—all of these things seem so much more real to us. Yet they offer us no true security.

There are people, however, for whom moments of quiet reflection are not foreign at all. And we note their deep commitment. It is reported that the great Reformer, Martin

Luther, prayed for three hours each day. He found time for silent meditation before he found time for his writing and speaking engagements. This left little doubt about his priorities.

In the the Old Testament, man was expected to offer to God his most perfect animal as a sacrifice. An animal that was defective and sickly was not acceptable. Perhaps this is a reminder that God wants nothing less than the best from us. The allocation of our time is one of the surest indicators of the real priorities in our lives.

A Place for Prayer

Jesus' words about a private quiet time suggests that a prayer life will be disciplined and regular ("when you pray"). There is also the suggestion that a quiet time occur in a place where we can meditate without distractions. "Go into your room and shut the door and pray to your Father who is in secret" (Matt. 6:6). The room Jesus mentions is, in the King James Version, the closet. That term signified the innermost room in the house, where disturbances were least likely. Here we are able to screen out all of the noises of the day and meditate in silence. Here we can allow our thoughts to become captive to the will of God.

For thousands of years the people of God have found strength in reading the Scriptures. Imagine as you read the Psalms that you share the psalmist's moments of tragedy and his moments of praise, for you share his faith. Or, as you read the gospel narratives about Jesus, draw resources for the day from the strength and character of his life. For a few minutes shut out the trivial words that come over the airwaves and listen to Jesus' majestic message in his Sermon on the Mount.

Many people find strength in reading the great spiritual classics or the great hymns which form a part of our heritage. Their words have stirred faithful people for generations. All of these resources provide strength for our daily lives and give us the stamina to endure the ordinary trials of life.

Jesus' Quiet Time

There is an illuminating passage in the Gospel of Luke, in which the disciples seemed to track down the mystery of Jesus' life. "What gave Jesus his enormous power and authority?" they seemed to ask. Someone might have pointed to his teachings as facts which made him different. Instead the disciples asked, "Lord, teach us to pray, as John taught his disciples" (Luke 11:1). They saw in his prayer life the power that made a difference.

On the Mount of Transfiguration Jesus spoke not only to God but also to Moses and Elijah (Luke 9:30–31). In the Garden of Gethsemane he prayed, "O my Father, if it be possible, let this cup pass from me" (Matt. 26:39, KJV). Early in his ministry he sent away the five thousand who thronged about him and told his disciples to set sail across the lake. Meanwhile, he walked back into the hills: "He went up into a mountain apart to pray: and when the evening was come, he was there alone" (Matt. 14:23, KJV).

At all of the great turning points in his life, Jesus prayed. Luke tells us that he was praying at the time of his baptism (Luke 3:21). He prayed all night before he chose his disciples (Luke 6:12). Finally, at Gethsemane, we hear his prayer, "Thy will . . . thy will." He had earlier taught his disciples to pray, "Thy will be done." In the crisis of his life, he himself prayed the same words: "Thy will be done" (Matt. 6:10; 26:42).

Many people remember Jesus for his teachings and for his works of healing. The whole world stands in awe of the majesty and clarity of the Sermon on the Mount. The authority with which he spoke has distinguished him from any other teacher. His miracles put him in a class by himself. But how do you explain his unique power? The disciples knew the secret; they said, "Teach us to pray." As George Buttrick has said, "His life and death had their secret springs, like a river back in the hills where he was wont to pray."

Resources for Living

Someone has made the rather ironic statement that the shorter and quicker our quiet time, the more of a burden it becomes. But our quiet time should be the spring from which our priorities flow. It should be the time we acknowledge and honor the Lord of our life, the place where we seek his guidance for our earthly journey.

I am reminded of Jesus' saying that "my yoke is easy and my burden is light" (Matt. 11:30). It sounds like a contradiction in terms to speak of a yoke being easy or a burden light. Yokes, after all, are placed on oxen in order to facilitate their work. But yokes also give direction and discipline to the oxen. In the same way Jesus' yoke gives discipline—badly needed discipline—to our lives. It is the same way with our quiet time. This discipline is not a burden. It suggests that we have found a direction in our lives.

Several years ago a young woman who was traveling in East Germany was arrested on the charge of helping East German citizens to escape. As she entered her confinement, she was a self-proclaimed agnostic. She had to endure the rounds with the interrogators, the idleness, and the menial labor imposed on her. Cut off from family and friends, she was totally without resources. In *Every Wall Shall Fall*, Hellen Battle tells how she looked out her window one day in spring and saw a beautiful blue sky. It occurred to her that, in the German language, the word *Himmel* means both "sky" and "heaven"—the place of God's presence. In her enforced quiet time, she began to find resources in prayer and Bible reading. Her tragic imprisonment began to give meaning and direction to her life. The world had been "too much with her" before.

We do not need to experience tragic events in order to enrich our lives. We can enter into our rooms and pray to our Father with the assurance that he will hear and answer our prayers. As we learn to spend more time in prayer and to trust in God more fully, we will find the help we need to survive the crises in our lives.